THE HST MODEL FOR CHANGE

Other books by Robert Brown

The People Side of Lean Thinking

Transparent Management

Lean Thinking 4.0

Earn Their Loyalty

Mistake-Proofing Leadership (with Rudy F. Williams)

New Darwinian Laws Every Business Should Know (with Patrick Edmonds)

Personal Wisdom

The Really Good Ideas Mini-Book Series

Simply Bob (a memoir)

First Ten Days in Heaven (a novel)

Things I Learned from My Wife

Youth Character Building Tool Kit

Invivo (a novel)

Mayhem at the Open (a novel)

Murder on the Tour (a novel)

The Golf Gods

The Way of Golf

The Golfing Mind

Golf Tips

THE HST MODEL FOR CHANGE

Enhancing the People Side of Organizational Development

Robert Brown

bp books

Cover design by Elm Street Design

Published by bp books
11700 Mukilteo Speedway #201-1084
Mukilteo WA 98275
USA

Printed in the United States of America

Library of Congress Control Number: 2016941038

Paper
ISBN-13: 978-0-9836768-7-4
ISBN-10: 0-9836768-7-9

Hardcover
ISBN-13: 978-0-9836768-9-8
ISBN-10: 0-9836768-9-5

To

John Kotter
Who shifted organizational change from head to heart

and

Roger A. Kaufman
Who inspired me and so many others

CONTENTS

The Fifty-Year Effort

Perhaps the most frightening four words in the English language are "We need to talk," especially when uttered by a woman to a man. These words can only mean something terrible is about to happen. Often the man is told there is a problem, a big problem, one that means he must change, or the relationship is over or worse, it is too late for him to change and the relationship *is* over.

Similar reactions occur when change is suggested at work. The same dread, the same fears, the same loss of control. Feelings of inadequacy and hurt race through the heart and soul of the worker.

When change is in the air, the divide between what is good for the organization and what is good for the employee widens. Employees feel disposable. The unknown becomes threatening. Trust is lost. Looking out for number one becomes a priority. The organization, and the people in it, often become lost.

Organizational development has created change models that

enable us to take the right steps, in the right order, and make change easier, faster, and more sustainable than before. But the commonly accepted estimate of about a thirty percent success rate suggests we have not yet identified the optimal method, if there is one.

HST begins with the most basic element of who we are: our biology. Improving our change efforts will not be done by assessing personality types, generational similarities or group adaptability, not even by better comprehending the quicksand of business culture. Effective change will happen by better understanding how our brains are hard-wired. From that fundamental biological reality, we can implement more realistic and effective people interactions to support organizational development.

"HST" stands for "Harnessing the Speed of Thought." This model initiates the change process where it actually begins, in the human brain, then expands outwards through teams and leaders to move the entire organization forward. By beginning with how the human brain works, this new model creates a direct path from a creative idea to discussions to decisions to implementing and then to sustaining change. It works by supporting critical people needs first, which then support business needs. You will learn how to set up the change process even before a change is contemplated and ensure buy-in by all strata of the organization.

However, the essential process of our change model is not a simple fix, because it is counterintuitive. It doesn't take longer, and it finds better solutions, but it alters how the brain naturally attacks problems. Superior results make the effort worthwhile.

Although the HST model for change includes measured and ordered steps, it must be adjusted to the realities of each organization, just as a chili recipe should be altered for different tastes. People who are interacting must be encouraged to contribute their perceptions and ideas for how the model should be applied. Models are tools and should not take precedence over people.

George Box (*Journal of the American Statistical Association*, 1976) adds this suggestion: "Since all models are wrong the scientist cannot obtain a 'correct' one by excessive elaboration. On the contrary, following William of Occam he should seek an economical description of natural phenomena."

Our model must be simple, clear, and logical. It must fit the people; the people should not be squeezed to fit the model. The HST model is a tool to enhance people interactions, not control them.

I'm excited to provide you with over fifty years of observing, trying, and learning so you can become a more successful change agent. The book is dedicated to John Kotter, with whom I had an email exchange a few years ago culminating in his invitation to lunch. We haven't had that lunch yet, but the dedication is my thanks for the invitation and his contribution to the field and my professional development.

It is also dedicated to one of my dissertation committee members, Roger A. Kaufman. My dissertation was based on his book describing educational planning, and his early support and teaching have guided much of what I have done with my career.

As presented in the third section, the HST model contains two essentials for organizational change. You can include whatever other essentials exist in your organization. This might be an investment in other approaches, following the guidance of an expert consultant or applying lessons brought back by inspired conference attendees.

Keep in mind that organizational development is not an unimpeded linear process. Don't expect change to always be upward like riding an escalator; it is more a hands-and-feet scramble up a slippery hillside.

In the HST model, a "leader" is anyone who has responsibility for others, and who is expected to make decisions regarding them. "Teams" are not groups of people working together but a group of individuals that has been trained to support each other moving toward an emotionally compelling goal.

Change does not need to be traumatic. It does not even need to be complicated. It can and should be exciting, enjoyable, and fulfilling. You just have to do it right. Our approach has one essential focus and two essential ingredients. It's as simple and effective a change model as I could create.

Where HST is being used, when someone says, "We need to talk," the most likely response might be, "Great! I have a lot of ideas."

THE HST MODEL FOR CHANGE

TRUST

The current 2020 coronavirus pandemic is an unfortunate example of the chaos of change. Health experts tell us wearing a mask affords an important degree of personal and public protection. In totalitarian countries, people have been dragged from their homes and arrested for not wearing a mask. Compliance in these environments can be demanded. In democracies, people declare, "This is a free country" and refuse to use a mask. Store owners say that they know more about what their customers need than the government. Some state governors mandate wearing masks and other governors do not, which it is depends less on medical science and more on political philosophy. Our response to the pandemic is confused, uneven, and, so far, less than effective.

World War II stressed our population is similar ways. Uncertainty pervaded daily life. Hardship was a certainty, death a possibility. Personal sacrifice was needed. Unlike now, most people during the war rallied, made the war effort a priority, and did what needed to be done.

What made the war effort different were three critical elements. One was the feeling that "We are all in this together." This sense of unity fostered all the characteristics of teamwork, from kids collecting tin to adult women no longer buying precious nylon but painting stockings on their legs. Car tires were patched, re-patched, and repatched again. Everyone was front and center doing their duty. President Roosevelt asked everyone for "equality of sacrifice." It became a patriotic duty and an honor to those on the home front to give up ration coupons for those in greater need.

The second element was the sense that the cause was righteous. We were the good guys. We were fighting for freedom. God was on our side. If not a sacred duty, it was close to it.

And third, the cost of failure would be catastrophic. American freedom was at risk as was the glorious experiment in democracy. More people will be enslaved, more people will be killed. Evil dictators would rule the world.

Trusting that these ideals were truths brought the country together.

Trust was almost universal for WWII and is much less so for the corona pandemic. Trust. Trust in leadership. Trust in the importance of the fight. Trust that the goal is the right one. Trust that we are all in this together. Trust that we will prevail.

These elements translate into the smaller world of organizational change. If we add one more concept, the core change dynamics of a business become clear. The concept is the Organization-Individual Divide (O-I) from *Transparent Management*, Brown, 2011. The O-I Divide is the insurmountable gap between what is good for the organization and what is good for the individual employee. The company always comes first. Countless individual lives have been devastated because the company found it had too many employees for current needs and dismissed the surplus. Or the company declares "our platform is on fire" and demands immediate and significant changes and sacrifices from its workers. Employees are "grist for the mill" whenever the mill needs grist, and they know it.

In business, trust must bridge the O-I divide. Employees must trust leadership and leadership must trust employees. Everyone must trust the problem is identified accurately and is one that must be addressed. The goal must be the right one and the method to reach it must be the best one.

If you focus on creating and maintaining trust, you will not need much, or anything, from popular change tools and ideas such as personality tests, overcoming resistance and the "change curve" and the "pit of despair." You will not have to worry about late adopters. These extras are not needed. Trust will mobilize everyone to do what needs to be done.

What matters is how completely the people affected are allowed to address the issue at hand. The HST model creates a process for effective people involvement. People can implement what is best for them and best for the company.

OD practitioners advocate using a four-step approach to improve organizations:

- Diagnosis
- Action planning
- Implementation
- Evaluation

With our model, we have taken the first two steps for you and hope our efforts will stimulate you to take the last two using the HST change model.

Our *diagnosis* is that organizations do not understand change and have been misled about how to do it well. This conclusion is based on so many organizations using extraneous tools, tests, and models and on the limited success they have when implementing change. As George Box suggests, our model will simplify the change process and focus on increasing trust of people and inclusively managing change.

Our *plan* is to improve how employees understand change and shepherd that enhanced awareness through two critical elements of an organization. Organizational development does not have to be traumatic. People are not incomprehensibly complicated. Focus on how best to create trust in every aspect of change.

The HST Model enables employees and leaders to transparently work through all the steps and issues of organizational change. Trust will grow at each step.

Information propels the initial surge, then trust takes the lead, closely followed by loyalty and effort. To make change work, you cannot do better than that.

THE TWO ESSENTIALS

To be successful, organizational change must make sense to all involved, from each employee to the organization as a whole. This book addresses these issues:

- How do we make sense of change?
- How do we make the *right* sense of change?
- Where in the organization do we have to make this happen?

Change is messy work, involves a lot of planning and effort, demands feedback loops, and fails if formulae and other lockstep methods are required. There is no one recipe for success. There are no five steps, seven steps, or twenty steps that will guarantee everyone will join the effort and that the effort will be successful.

That being said, however, there is an effective way to understand change and an effective way to improve the chances of successful change.

There are two HST model for change essentials. Think of them as glue, an epoxy of resin and hardener first to make change possible and then to make change stick.

The Two HST Change Essentials

- Change must make logical and emotional sense *from beginning to end* to everyone involved
- Change must be guided through teams and leaders

Most change efforts do not fulfill their promise, and it's probably true that thirty percent or less of company improvements meet expectations. You can do better. It is not rocket science. To paraphrase Peter Drucker, good leadership and similarly, good change management, can and should be done by ordinary people, not geniuses or super-leaders. You will need to pay attention to reality, appreciate individual differences, avoid pretending to know something when you don't, listen more than talk, keep things transparent, and widely broadcast successes and failures as you go. That isn't often done.

While working on this book, I had coffee with a friend who told me her CEO emailed all employees that her local company was merging with a large international firm. "Merging?" I asked. She said yes, and that no changes would take place for at least two years. I read in the business section of the local paper the next day that my friend's company had been bought and the international buyer had big plans. A few weeks after our conversation, my friend said that some executives from the larger company took a tour of her workplace. They smiled and nodded at all they saw, said nothing, and were gone within thirty minutes. Months after the email announcement and the visit, there has been no further word from management about the merger. No information in this situation leads to anxiety. My friend, an older employee who loves her job, is now thinking about finding a new one; she fears that since she loves her company and her position, change can only be negative, and since she might have trouble being hired elsewhere, now is a good time to look. This is irritating to hear, ridiculously common and worse, unnecessary. I want to share the HST change model to improve how change is managed to save people like my friend and to help organizations such as yours.

It's as simple as building trust, making sense emotionally and logically, and making changes through teams led by competent leaders.

LOGICAL AND EMOTIONAL SENSE

COGS IN THE WHEEL

Cogs and wheels are necessities in many machines and have also proved to be a useful metaphor for modern organizations. The turning wheel is the business organization, and the cogs are the people doing the work. It's a useful metaphor because a company wants standardization, predictability, uniformity, and the like to run smoothly. We do that for good reason: we think it is efficient. And it *is* efficient until you want to change things.

The Cogs

It's not so bad being a cog in the corporate wheel; we get stability, reasonable certainty, security, understandable career paths, and clear job descriptions. For many, being a secure cog in a prosperous wheel is a fair tradeoff. Can such a cog be an asset to an organization seeking change? To answer that, let's explore two human components employees bring through the doors every workday: their mental and emotional selves. These two components overlap, converge, collide and change by the second and are, to date, not well understood. There are many theories of personality; a perhaps equal number of social psychology concepts; solid evidence for learning theories; well-documented behavior motivators; growing evidence of how eighty billion brain neurons convert chemicals to thoughts and feelings; and for some theorists, a universal human quest for meaning in life. Effective organizational change does not require us to become experts in any of this. We don't have to know much, but we have to know something.

Mental

This is where most people are off-base in what they think they know. We all subscribe to an erroneous assumption and don't realize it, so here is the truth: the human brain was not designed to be logical. It was designed by the soft yet lethal hand of evolution for species survival, nothing less and nothing more. Any threatening or potentially threatening situation evokes a quick response, one that is often unconscious. The primary purpose of the biological brain is twofold:

1. *To keep us alive*:
   We make some decisions that are a function of our hereditary makeup and others based on personal experience. What worked before we assume will work again, since we're still alive and that's a good enough outcome. If there is a change in our environment that we don't understand, this is a threat, and our brain says it is bad. (Which is not good for trust.)

2. *To get our genes into the gene pool*:
    If another person appears welcoming, we are attracted
    to the person and are liable to do illogical things and en-
    ter dicey situations. Whatever logic we have flies out the
    window when an attractive opportunity—perhaps a
    possible mate, perhaps just a good time—flutters our
    way.

As we shall see, when individuals gather to solve a problem or
promote a change, few if any are applying logic the way they
think they are. We know about people having a range of IQs and
we even talk about the role of EQ, emotional intelligence. What
we don't talk about and don't realize is how poorly our brains
co-ordinate with other brains. Individual brains make quick and
good-enough decisions. A group of brains ends up voting which
kneejerk and good-enough solution is the best one. This is one
reason change efforts are unsuccessful. Making logical sense of
change is next to impossible if those promoting the change 1)
don't use sufficient logic to decide on changes and 2) don't communicate in ways that make logical sense. However, if the
change and presentation of change make logical sense, our
brains will rejoice with a flood of pleasing neurochemicals.

Emotional

We think we have a handle on this too, but we don't. Can we
leave our troubles at the door of the workplace as we're expected to? Of course not. Do we all respond to emotional stimuli

the same way? No again. Do we know where emotions come from? Not really. Do we know the best way to cope with emotions? No.

Do we have only four emotions as some say: happy, sad, surprised, and angry? Or is this a better list:

- Curiosity
- Indifference
- Desire
- Fear
- Sorrow
- Frustration
- Pride
- Sympathy
- Hate

- Panic
- Surprise
- Hope
- Rage
- Gratitude
- Joy
- Jealousy
- Love
- Boredom

Emotionally, we are a complex species.

Another way we can look at our emotional selves is that we are motivated by physical drives (think food and sex). We also respond to reward and punishment. We seek a feeling of dignity and value. Most of us seek companionship, a bit of fun, and a chance to kick back sometimes. Our emotions are varied, wide-ranging, and powerful, and are likely the primary reason change is not as successful as it could be. How is an organization supposed to take into account the almost infinite range of emotions brought into work every day? They will not be easy to include, but emotions drive what we do and are why making emotional sense of change is so critical.

The Cogs and the Wheel

Individuals who work together must mesh somehow into an effective work unit, no matter their mental and emotional functioning. This is usually done through rules and regulations, company policies, sharp-eyed supervisors, job descriptions, tolerance for bad habits, and the like. We take unique people and—with no, little or erroneous information—clump them into what we furtively hope is a team or, more likely, we settle for a functional workgroup. I think what happens is we figuratively stick employees to a wheel with bubble gum and use them as cogs until they fall off for one reason or another and we find someone to take their place and chew on more bubble gum until we have enough to stick the new employees on the wheel too.

We need these unique individuals to come to work every day and on time, and to put aside their personal needs for the benefit of the company. Once these people settle in and get a comfortable rhythm going, it seems disruptive to insist on making changes. It isn't asking too much; we're just lousy at it. People are changing all the time and want to. We like driving a new car. We like acquiring new skills and developing our hobbies. There isn't anything much better than discovering a great vacation spot, a new favorite restaurant, or bringing a newborn home to the family. Few of us would turn down a job promotion. Anyone who says people do not like change is wrong. Use yourself as an example and recall your latest electronics purchase, or how important your golf lessons are or how much time you spent shopping for your latest outfit. We seek change; we embrace change… if done right.

People are the Problem

We modern humans have had about seventy thousand years to figure out how to work together. Although it is tempting to blame our limited success on the small portion of our genome coming from Neanderthals, we must take personal responsibility for our strengths and weaknesses and improve both.

We are quick to identify problems in processes but slow to recognize our personal deficits in how we understand ourselves and interact with others. As a species, we are not as elevated as we think we are. Our technology often outpaces our morality. We believe we are above other living things. Compared to other mammals, including most other great apes, we are sex maniacs. We kill each other in large numbers, in brutal ways, and with extreme efficiency. A huge percentage of natural resources are depleted by our growing list of indulgences and burgeoning population. We have a hard time choosing between short-term (e.g. quarterly profits or personal comfort) and long-term (e.g. planetary health) goals.

We're not so hot in more individual ways. We don't listen well. We make bad assumptions and jump to wrong conclusions. Judging others is almost automatic and often subconscious. We debate more than we discuss. Some people irritate us, while others are boring. Instead of using our excess energy to build a habitat for humanity, we work out at the gym. Half of us are fat.

It takes a lot of effort to change our biological perceptions and attitudes. We believe what was good yesterday is good today and most likely will be good tomorrow. We also believe that others can't have our best interests in mind. How can they know for sure what's good for us? Someone making a change that affects me is suspected of having ulterior motives not in my best interest until proven otherwise. And the benefit of change proposed by others is often not rewarded in proportion to my personal effort and personal cost of the change. Change pulls the rug out of my comfort zone. Boredom is preferable to anxiety. Change can only be good if it lessens my discomfort or otherwise makes my life more enjoyable, and you have to prove that before I'm willing to make a move without being forced. With building blocks like these, how is a business supposed to improve?

Change isn't the problem. Resistance to change isn't the problem either. The people problem with organizational change is that from the perspective of most of those affected, the change doesn't make logical and emotional sense and certainly is not to be trusted. It's as simple as that.

Of course, what makes sense to me might not make sense to you, and what makes sense to the company might not make sense to the person being laid off.

Our approach to organizational development asserts that effective change, sustainable change, must make logical and emotional sense to everyone. One global point of view, the type found in corporate talking points, won't get the job done. There are as many human realities as there are employees, and those realities are constantly changing. Joe might be a happy-go-lucky employee—until he gets married, until he has a child, until he hurts his back. Jill might love her job—until her mentor/boss leaves the company, until her hours change, until her bus route adds four extra miles and eleven extra stops.

People are the Solution

We are slow at changing, even for our physical well-being. It took the British navy almost half a century to apply the cure for scurvy that James Lind, one of their physicians, discovered. We're still having trouble knocking out polio in parts of the world because a few people are against the effort. Too many infections are caused by doctors and nurses failing to wash their hands often enough. Change isn't easy, but we can change and do change, so change is possible and possible to do better, even in the workplace.

People will not resist if a change makes logical *and* emotional sense. Such dual sense would prevent human follies such as smoking cigarettes to look cool, throwing rocks and bombs at people who are different, and not wearing masks during a pandemic.

Business faces this challenge:

> *Every change in every part of the organization must make logical and emotional sense to every employee throughout the entire change process.*

Note these factors.

- The change must make sense to the employee's feeling of well-being
- Emotions are more important in change than the facts
- Everyone is different and has different expectations and needs
- Different company strata and divisions also have different expectations and needs
- Compliance is of little value—acceptance must become commitment
- Being involved in the full process of change makes a significant difference
- Peer group acceptance is a powerful force

Making sense of change means: the change is in my best interest; it can be accomplished; the cost/benefit to me is positive; if the change is not made, bad things will happen.

Change does not make sense when: I don't understand the problem or opportunity being addressed; I don't know what the outcome will be; the cost/benefit to me is unknown or negative; I don't trust the people promoting the change; the change doesn't seem to be the right one; my peer group is against it; it seems like change for change's sake.

Back to the Wheel

Think of an organization as a giant slow-moving wheel in all of its possible configurations: corporate culture, the tenor of meetings, range of supervisor competencies, company vision and mission, openness, and everything else, good and bad, that makes up what employees experience in the workplace.

Most places are decent enough. Employees aren't quitting in droves or filing complaints with the local DA's office. Companies do their best to conduct themselves so the business thrives, and employees receive a paycheck. Fortunately, most employees are happy to do the work, fit in with others, not rock the boat, and otherwise support the status quo. Few new hires are told to enhance their job so that in six months they will be doing something different. No. The organizational wheel must revolve in predictable ways at the right speed with no wobbles. Not doing the job as defined creates wobbles. That's a problem in most places. Employees are told to do their jobs as well as they can and that variations will have consequences, few of them happy ones.

What kind of wheel would promote change? One that was in danger. A business crisis supports change, especially one demanding immediate action or the company will cease to function. People can get behind a change like that. But what about an organization that isn't in crisis? What if a company just wants to improve?

A large wheel has momentum, not agility. There is something better. Think about it this way. A racing bicycle has multiple gears; this means multiple wheels with different diameters and cogs so the rider can change gears (wheels and cogs) as hills and valleys are encountered. Organizations aren't built that way. They seem to have one giant wheel (defined by some as corporate culture) and permanent cogs.

So-called "nimble" companies are a little different and seem to be able to change gears quickly, and matrix companies, at their best, also act like multiple wheels with varying cogs. The idea is to avoid sticking employees to a giant wheel and keeping them spinning in the same direction and at the same rate for eternity until suddenly we want to change something.

A company that endorses change and is successful at initiating and sustaining change is like a collection of different sized wheels where employees hop on and off as necessary to keep the wheels rolling. Ideally, employees jump on and off voluntarily, as needed, when needed. Every change can be a new wheel: big ones, small ones, fast ones, and even slow ones.

Organizational development is easier if it is more like changing gears than it is changing a giant tire in a cold rain, in the dark, and with a flashlight that only works if you shake it just right.

An attractive manifestation of cogs and wheels is team members and teams. Imagine being a backup quarterback rushing in for the injured star and throwing the pass that wins the game. Or how about being a stand-in ballerina saving the show? Or how about being an employee asked to join an important task force? Not cogs but members. Not wheels but teams, teams that know how to work together to achieve success. That's the HST model for change.

WHY THE HST MODEL WORKS

My dissertation back in '73 was a system analysis of psychotherapy. The concept was that people change from being distressed to being healthy through a series of steps, and I wanted to identify what those steps were and how to measure them. My assumption was that psychotherapy was a form of education where the patient learned how to go from a bad state to a good state. I researched various types of therapies and theories, found an educational template I could try (*Educational System Planning*, Roger Kaufman, 1972) and created a model for individual change. The model included determining needs, a mission analysis, function analysis, task analysis, and a method-means analysis. I ended up with a multi-page flow diagram and a way of initiating and monitoring change. My last task was to compare the model to successful therapy. Happily, it fit and I was awarded the degree. It was hailed as a potential landmark work at the time

A few years later, while practicing health psychology with most of my patients referred by their physicians, I noticed a significant disconnect between many of the patients and their doctors.

As part of my investigation of this problem, I reviewed my original doctoral research focusing on determining needs. According to Professor Kaufman, needs are often misconstrued as what we need to do, such as "we need to hire more workers to meet customer demand." Instead, he insisted that "need" should be a noun, not a verb, and be defined as the gap between current outcomes and desired or required outcomes. For example, a need could be "Our current production meets only half of our customer demand."

The fulcrum of the HST model is understanding that "need" is not an action but a gap.

It is a confounding human mental trait that we confuse and often combine *what* we want to achieve with *how* we want to achieve it. How that gap is defined begins the HST change process.

The physicians were focused on health while patients were concerned about many things, including denial of a medical problem, wanting to feel in control, and even resisting the spouse who first recognized the problem. My challenge was to get the doctor and patient to define the same need (gap) so they could work together. Over a couple of years in the late 1970s, I distilled my dissertation's hundred pages of flow diagrams, measures, and methods into six steps to understand and solve problems. These steps were:

1. Identify the problem
2. Define the goal in measurable terms
3. List hurdles or constraints
4. List possible solutions
5. Choose the best solution
6. Revise as needed

I taught this method to patients and their doctors so they could begin at step one to define problems mutually—that is, to understand and agree to the physical and emotional gaps they faced. Some docs saw this process as beyond what they should be expected to do. They were physicians, they said, not babysitters or psychotherapists. In their view, medical reasons for change should be enough. If patients resisted, they were bad patients. I was viewed as a necessary interface, the person responsible for using psychological tools to enable patients to follow medical treatment plans.

At the same time, I began doing more business consulting focused on customer service, improving employee morale, and helping leaders lead. I noticed a similar disconnect between management and labor as existed between doctor and patient. Leadership's problem analysis often meant implementing a new strategy when few if any employees knew of any issues. On some occasions, leaders ignored the personnel needs I identified. However, when I applied the six steps with management and labor, it worked. Problems were addressed and solved.

Over time I continued to distill this model until it became:

1. Define the issue (problem or opportunity)
2. Define the goal in measurable terms
3. List hurdles/concerns
4. List possible solutions
5. Choose the best solution

I omitted "revise as needed" because revisions should occur at each step as a dynamic way of improving the accuracy of problem-solving. The model continued to solve a wide range of problems and conflicts among people.

It's common knowledge that different people observe and interpret things differently, so one of the next additions to enhance the HST model was to coin what I called the Four Billion Rule, based on the then world population of four billion people. The rule has since grown into the Seven Billion Rule and says: *At first, everyone will always see everything differently.* So the intent of this new model, to define the problem or opportunity mutually, is that everyone arrives at the same definition of the issue and its significance.

That first step is critically important. The gap has to be agreed to by all parties, must be viewed as an issue that is important enough to be addressed and also defined without sneaking in a solution.

But why are the next steps necessary? People have been solving problems together for thousands of generations. Shouldn't agreeing on the problem or opportunity be enough? The answer comes from neuroscience. In his book *What is Thought?* Eric Baum explains how the brain approaches problems. Summarizing basic research, he concludes that the brain has evolved biological processes to quickly and efficiently find solutions. As mentioned earlier, these brain processes assume that what worked before will most likely work again. Why bother creating something new? Just apply the solution that worked in a similar situation. Another book, *Thinking, Fast and Slow* by Daniel Kahneman, further explained how the brain uses simplifying templates. The human brain races to already proven solutions pretty much unconsciously. *Blink,* by Malcolm Gladwell, emphasizes the usefulness of trusting this quick response to a problem and provides examples of when it works and when it doesn't. Bottom line? When faced with a problem, the brain takes the line of least resistance. Nothing in our makeup seeks the optimal solution, and we may only stumble upon it when debating options. People working together to solve problems can improve their efficiency and effectiveness by slowing the problem-solving process and managing it properly.

Organizations run into difficulty because of the human instinct to race toward solutions. Instinctive mental shortcuts use old patterns of thought and often reinforce status quo responses. An already-been-chewed solution comes to mind rather than the best one. A handful of people trying to agree on a course of action debate solutions their brains pulled out of storage. Large groups become a cognitive mob, and an entire organization is bedlam. Experts in OD have created models to cope with, but not overcome, this madness.

The HST model works by slowing the brain's dash to a good-enough solution and externalizing it so people solving problems can see what they are doing and work together to *assemble* the best solution. It worked well for individuals to solve problems and for groups of people to solve problems. It also does well helping an organization's development.

Many organizational change models provide guidance: Kotter's eight steps (sense of urgency, guiding coalition, vision, a volunteer army, remove barriers, short-term wins, sustain acceleration, institute change), Bridges' Transition model (endings, neutral zone, new beginnings), Prosci's ADKAR model (awareness, desire, knowledge, ability, reinforcement), General Electric's CAP (Change, Acceleration, Process) and even Lewin's venerable unfreeze, change and refreeze.

These models all have something to offer and they work, to varying degrees, to foster change in organizations. But none of them addresses the neurological mental framework we bring to work every day. Understanding and overcoming the consequences of the simplifying brain and the Seven Billion Rule would make organizational change easier and more effective.

Organizational change has never been easy. The difficulty begins with how we hastily and unconsciously solve problems via hard-wired neural pathways and is made worse by inadequate communication of individual thoughts and our natural tendency to resist what we don't understand or agree with. If we used our inherent brainpower more effectively and communicated more understandably, many of the problems we encounter in organizational development would no longer exist, and we wouldn't be tempted to apply so many layers of psychosocial bandages.

The HST model for change recognizes how individuals, groups, and organizations solve problems. Individuals solve problems in the simplest and quickest way possible. Groups solve problems by *debating* issues and solutions. Organizations solve problems by using models to persuade people into making changes someone insists they have to.

A better way is to use Harnessing the Speed of Thought to guide our thinking and our group problem-solving.

On the next page is a diagram of the HST model.

Harnessing the Speed of Thought

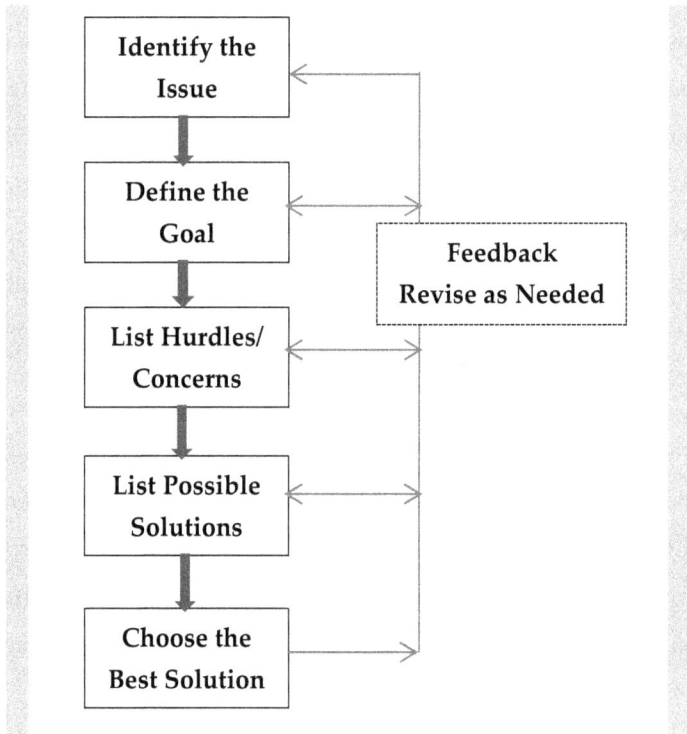

```
┌──────────────┐
│ Identify the │ ←─────────────┐
│    Issue     │               │
└──────┬───────┘               │
       │                       │
┌──────▼───────┐               │
│  Define the  │ ←─────────┐   │
│     Goal     │           │   │    ┌──────────────────────┐
└──────┬───────┘           │   │    │       Feedback        │
       │                   │   │    │   Revise as Needed    │
┌──────▼───────┐           │   │    └──────────────────────┘
│ List Hurdles/│ ←─────────┤   │
│   Concerns   │           │   │
└──────┬───────┘           │   │
       │                   │   │
┌──────▼───────┐           │   │
│ List Possible│ ←─────────┤   │
│   Solutions  │           │   │
└──────┬───────┘           │   │
       │                   │   │
┌──────▼───────┐           │   │
│  Choose the  │ ─────────►│   │
│ Best Solution│               │
└──────────────┘               │
```

Everyone involved works on identifying the problem or opportunity and doesn't move to defining the goal until everyone agrees that the identified issue is the right one to address. The same is true for the goal. Everyone agrees to the goal and how it should be measured before moving to hurdles. Hurdles to be overcome and concerns to be addressed are listed until no more can be identified. Possible solutions are listed until no more can be thought of. The possible solutions are compared to the goal and hurdles to choose which solution best overcomes hurdles and reaches the goal. If no solution works, then either the goal has to be altered or insurmountable hurdles become new issues to be addressed before the original issue can be solved.

This model can design small projects, outline corporate merger strategies, and help committees get their work done. There are other problem-solving models. The Shewhart cycle (PDCA) is popular: plan, do, check, act. Education Business Articles promotes another five-step effort: identify the problem, identify the plan, identify what might happen, work the strategy, and measure. Small business supporter Chron has a five-stepper too: identify the problem, describe the cause, brainstorm solutions, implement the solution, and monitor your solution. On the Yale education website, a six-step process was presented: define the problem, determine root cause, develop alternative solutions, select a solution, implement the solution, evaluate the outcome. Even the Lean Thinking A3 form has similar elements.

These models bury the goal into one step or another. A strength of HST is to emphasize the goal as a major element. The HST model works well because:

1. There is an emphasis on a mutually defined and measurable issue, and each step is worked on by everyone at the same time until agreeing that the step has been

completed. This emphasis almost automatically creates trust and our desired team environment.

2. The goal is defined mutually and becomes emotionally engaging. (builds trust)

3. Individual concerns are sought and recognized. (also builds trust)

4. The model externalizes and makes visual how the team can assemble solutions rather than debate them, a counterintuitive approach that makes a significant difference. (more trust)

5. The HST change model can fit into various steps of every other model. (extends the breadth of trust)

6. The model emphasizes and incorporates the basic human functions of thinking and feeling. (trust)

7. HST slows and externalizes an otherwise lightning-quick and invisible process. (ditto)

Employees must make sense of change from the onset, and the more this can be done together, the better. People are no longer cogs in wheels but members of teams. This is accomplished by enabling team members to identify the issues, define desired outcomes, list concerns, find possible solutions, and help to decide what change to implement.

Our working assumption is that normal brain processing complicates change and HST ensures this brain functioning is accommodated. Now we must move to the larger entity, the organization. We seek to help employees to own the problem, the process of change, and the new processes and outcomes.

We can best meet this challenge by keeping the process uncontaminated—that is, avoiding added layers of pseudoscientific and unnecessary tools and assumptions that hide the authentic nature of the people who come to work. Employees are people: people who seek a sense of safety and control; people who like security, enjoy success and want to feel that tomorrow will be okay; people who are frustrated by less than competent leadership and less than competent coworkers; people who want to leave work, go home to enjoy a good meal and play with the kids and, with just maybe experience a bit of meaning in their lives. The further from these core truths company change efforts wander, the more likely change will fail.

The simpler we can make organizational change, the better it will be. The more concrete and observable we can make change, the better. And the more change makes logical and emotional sense, the better it will be too.

GUIDING CHANGE

TEAMS AND LEADERS

Russell Wilson is a National Football League quarterback for the Seattle Seahawks. After a recent victory, he said, "We were superior in all aspects. We played for each other. We had fun. We got the job done." That is the dynamic we seek for organizational development. Football players make changes every week to prepare for new opponents on Sunday. They practice together to hone their teamwork. They study what they do well and not so well and work to improve. Coaches do their best to help each player do his best.

Football is only a game, a relatively simple game with only eleven players from each team on the field at any one time. The game lasts sixty minutes. A business is much more complex. It lasts eight or more hours a day and as far as I've seen, we don't practice anything. Studying might entail sitting at a computer completing mandatory courses as quickly as possible. For most businesses, organization means consistency and predictability. To many change experts, employees burrow into their roles and tasks, resisting change as if walls would crumble and their children starve if something, anything, were altered.

These experts have identified the major reasons businesses and employees resist change:

- Cultures are rigid
- Politics make change a war
- Fear of the unknown
- No payoff or reward for the effort
- People are invested in and like the old way
- They don't understand the need
- There could be a loss of status and/or jobs
- Fear of failure or poor performance in the new way
- They're not included in the process

All these elements and more come into play and affect change initiation and sustainability. Some experts proclaim that resistance to change is as inevitable as change itself. We know better. All this gnashing of teeth and wringing of hands is unnecessary. HST addresses all the above.

The people side of organizational development means that change must make logical and emotional sense if you want to build trust and change without demoralizing employees, spending a fortune, or taking forever to do it. The broader the change the greater the effort that must be made to include everyone in the right ways. Making logical and emotional sense at the organization level is the same as for individuals; after all, the organization is a collection of people.

The five steps of the HST model enable employees to make logical and emotional sense of change as each step is taken. The goal, for example, must be emotionally compelling. Frustrations and personal needs can be listed in the hurdles step. Facts and feelings are included and made public throughout the model. This is the first change essential. Now we should understand how to guide organizational development through teams and leaders. Our goal is an organization where change is a constant, where people seek change and embrace it. We should create a place where change means improvement in every way: improved effectiveness, improved efficiency, a better bottom line, excellent job satisfaction, and an increasing sense of personal value for all involved.

This can best be achieved through the efforts of real teams led by people who know how to build and sustain real teams.

TEAMS

High-performing teams are the most powerful force to ensure successful change; such teams are the headwaters of trust. Change can be implemented and sustained without teams, but that is like rowing a boat across the Atlantic through ten-foot swells rather than flying first class and sipping a favorite beverage along the way. Team elements include much of what is necessary for individuals to pull together to make something work, whether that something is old, new, or uncertain.

Every study of teams I have seen documents that teams are superior in every way to workgroups. Like many before me, I'm comfortable declaring that every employee should be on a team. It has also been my experience that the great majority of employees are in workgroups and not on teams. Why wouldn't you form teams where you work? Teams are not only more productive than workgroups, but they are also more enjoyable and rewarding for the members.

Early in my career, I worked with Olympic and professional sports teams. I noticed the complications when skilled and motivated athletes are expected to suppress personal glory for the good of the team. Selfish thinking is even more likely and problematic for employees unless they are members of a high-performing team.

There are team-building models you could use, including Tuckerman's venerable four stages of forming, storming, norming and performing, and Drexler and Sibbet's seven elements of orientation, trust-building, goal clarification, commitment, implementation, high-performance and renewal, and other models. Using one will make team-building much easier. My favorite is Rudy Williams' Four-Part Teaming Model.

Four-Part Teaming Model

1. Compelling Task	2. Sense of Membership
4. Personal Reward	3. Influence on Team

All of these elements enhance trust. If any are missing or underdeveloped, the team is weaker and less functional and is likely a workgroup playing at being a team. We will explore what each part entails and then examine how teams can be created and sustained.

1. Compelling Task

Athletic teams want to win the game; Navy Seal teams want to achieve their objective; work teams want to reach the goal. For all these teams, the outcome is imperative, that is, important enough for each team member to work hard to reach the goal. Without a compelling task, the work is ordinary and there is little need for a team; cogs in a wheel will get the work done well enough. A compelling task invites emotional engagement, one where the team effort is more important than striving for individual goals. A task is compelling if the problem or opportunity is significant. It is compelling if the goal makes logical and emotional sense.

The task does not have to be earth-shattering, heroic, or even interesting—just compelling. Some tasks may be only as compelling as taking out the kitchen garbage before it stinks. They can also be as grand as saving a life.

A compelling task can be any of the HST steps. The task can be to identify among all the issues at hand which one is the most critical to address. For example, "Staff satisfaction has dropped twenty percent over the last two years." It might be compelling for employees to investigate this finding and define a critical gap.

Just as easily, the task can be to define a goal, list hurdles, or find a solution.

Those involved in these activities are making sense of possible changes and are creating the first element of a high-performing team, identifying compelling tasks. Emotional engagement at this step is essential.

What adds gravitas to a compelling task is the possibility of victory or defeat. Fail to take out the garbage one evening and you will suffer the unpleasantness of a stinky morning kitchen. If you have skin in the game, if you win or lose, if your teammates rejoice or suffer with you, you care about the outcome and your teammates. This element is obvious with sports teams and rare in workgroups. The significance of results adds meaning to the activity.

If a change is important enough to do, there is some risk, some chance of failure, and with failure hurt to the organization. The team should feel the pain if it does not succeed. This does not mean the consequences of failure should be Draconian; internal distress is sufficient.

When people care, they are willing and often able to do whatever it takes to succeed. Success is often achieved solely by hard work and the unceasing effort to overcome adversity. Such emotional engagement can be established through the team's compelling task, and later enhanced through the sense of belonging on a team, the personal reward for making a team effort, and by being a part of a movement led by an esteemed leader.

We must elicit team unity through a compelling task, nurture these emotions, and not demean or dismiss them. Emotional engagement, for example, is strained when an organization inappropriately disciplines teams or individuals for making mistakes. There is anxiety about doing a good job, or at least, staying out of trouble. Such fear may lead to fewer mistakes (maybe) but surely leads to covering up errors. When the emotional context of the worker or team is self-preservation, correctly doing the task comes in second to pleasing the boss and a distant third to focusing on the outcome rather than improving anything. Outcomes can be and often are reached through less than honest and honorable efforts, and sometimes at a cost to coworkers. This self-preserving emotional state can arise in a punitive environment, a highly competitive one, one where everything is measured or one where rewards are individual rather than team-based. It is much easier to develop a workplace that is not emotionally engaging than one that is. It's an inverse correlation: the more top-down control, the less team emotional engagement. Sports teams and military units fighting for victory are notable exceptions but further support our contention of the power of a compelling task to enable teams and initiate change.

However, the greater the emotional engagement, the more stress for all involved. It is not a calm, easygoing workplace when passions are aroused. People will speak their minds, fight for what they believe is right, and otherwise confront the opposition, whoever and whatever it is. What leader wants more difficult to control workers? We should examine the downside of engagement in a compelling task.

First, engaged teams may be more affected when things are not going well, such as frustration with multiple barriers to change, most notably bureaucratic ones. Second, there is a cost to supporting engagement, more effort by the organization, more demands placed on managers, and more intense relationships with peers. Third, team members with greater engagement and the resultant greater sense of contribution and well-being may be the first ones to leave to make even greater contributions elsewhere. All factors considered, however, studies conclude that team engagement is best for the bottom line and best for the good of the employee.

Teams that feel they own the process and the outcome are the most engaged. Teams cannot own the process or the outcome if the change is not under their control. Even if the change makes logical and emotional sense, change directed by outside forces weakens emotional engagement and over time can eliminate it. Engagement arises in part from the mutual effort. If necessary, leadership can define the compelling task from its point of view and ask for help in getting the job done. When people are asked to help with something they deem important, they care, and when they care, they're emotionally engaged.

Engagement also requires progress. Toil by itself does little to build engagement. There must be a sense of movement. Additional structured team-building and sustaining after defining a compelling task increases engagement. Do this by making sure the task remains compelling and the members of the team are still the right members, and that team interactions and rewards are still effective.

A sense of meaning increases engagement. Does the effort, does the change, increase value in meaningful ways? A task that reduces the time to do the work by three percent is not as compelling as a task that makes the customer happier and adds to the sense of pride in the worker, and, if looking at the bigger picture (what my mentor Roger Kaufman calls "meta goals"), improves the world.

Understanding the why of a task increases engagement, particularly through a story. A few years ago, I was running a leadership workshop where we were exploring communication tools. Our focus at the time was telling difficult truths. I told the story of an airliner crash in 1977 on Tenerife, one of the Canary Islands. The runway was closed because of fog, and the captain of a KLM jumbo jet was anxious to get the plane airborne before his crew exceeded their work hours limit. Assuming he had takeoff clearance, the captain pushed the throttle forward. Junior members of the crew were afraid to contradict him. Halfway down the runway, almost at takeoff speed, the fog cleared enough for the crew to see a Pan Am jumbo jet crossing in front of them. The KLM cut through its middle. An avoidable crash that killed 583 people was caused by fog, impatience, and two men in the cockpit afraid to speak up. The resulting discussion by the workshop participants was intense and improving company communication became a compelling task. An emotionally laden story helps to increase engagement and motivation

An individual who feels a sense of belonging is engaged. This comes from being involved in something bigger than the individual. I recall working at a health care organization whose vision was "to be the quality leader." That was nice, I thought, but it didn't do much for my engagement. When we became a Lean Thinking organization, the vision changed to "be the quality leader and to transform health care." That got my blood flowing. I wanted to be a part of transforming health care.

A compelling task and the resultant emotional engagement is the fuel of successful change. By itself it is almost strong enough to power change; find a compelling task and get out of the way. The remaining three parts of Rudy's model, however, strengthen team functioning and ensure reaching the finish line and beyond.

2. Sense of Membership

Membership on a team is strongest if it is conditional, not automatic. Part of the reason workgroups are not stellar performers is that anyone in attendance is in the mix. Some in a workgroup make substantial contributions, while others show up only for the pizza.

Members of a team find the task compelling and want to contribute to the team's ability to complete the task. No one is on the team who doesn't belong. The effect on individual team members is strong when they know that other team members are committed and will contribute their best. If I know you bring something important to the team and thus belong on the team, and you know I bring something important and thus also belong, we are forming the core of a high-performing team. As far as change is concerned, we've already made an emotional commitment to the task, now we are making an emotional commitment to each other, and can act on it in ways that make logical sense.

One important consequence of both membership and influence on the team parts of the model is peer accountability. When coworkers depend on you, the individual is not just one person doing a job. You have people responsibility. Teammates have made a commitment to one another and each must ensure that others do what is necessary to get the job done. Peer accountability is why being on a team is such a valuable component of the workplace. Most places, this responsibility is absent or deficiencies in others are identified only to make trouble for them.

Supporting change is almost automatic in this element of teams. The sense each team member has is "I am an important part of the work, I am responsible in part for our success, and I am accountable to everyone else on the team." Each team member will give and receive feedback for improvement. Every team member will look for easier and better ways to reach the goal. There is the agreement that each team member will give whatever it takes to get the job done.

When I first learned Rudy's model, I thought the sense of membership was simply being identified as a member of a team. To me, everyone on the team wearing identical hats was enough. It took me a while to realize how wrong I was. Cogs in wheels can wear hats; real team members have much greater involvement and commitment. By joining the team, members understand their personal responsibility for team success. They publicly, and perhaps symbolically, declare that the team and the organization can count on them. This dynamic is profound. I may be a jerk. I may be a drunk. I may run around on my spouse, but when the team needs me, in any and every way it needs me, I will be there. Team needs take priority. For example, when behavior affects team morale, such as showing up late for meetings, the member will change that behavior for the benefit of the team or will no longer be on the team.

Only people who are the best contributors to the team can be on the team. Think of tryouts, such as baseball, theater companies, and even job interviews. People earn their way to team membership. A team that accepts or tolerates weak or noncontributing members is saying the task is not important and that failure is acceptable. This decreases the motivation of contributing members and isn't good for anyone. High-performing teams do not accept underperforming members and eject those who cease to contribute; that's what keeps them high performing.

However, the reality in the workplace is that members of a team will contribute varying degrees of value to the team effort. Not everyone will be a star; even on the New York Yankees, some players sit on the bench. Teams can handle performance variations by:

- Finding the member a different team
- Matching the team role to the limited abilities of the team member
- Creating an improvement plan to meet team needs and boost team roles as the person improves

The worst response is to allow poor performance to continue to be nice to the individual. The team must be more important than any team member or subgroup of members.

The sense of membership part of the Four-Part Teaming Model is the easiest to understand once you get over buying the same cap for everyone and accept that membership depends on contribution and the necessity of each member's awareness of his and others' value to the team.

It is the most difficult part of the model to achieve in the real world of the workplace.

3. Influence on the Team

To function well, team members must define how they will interact with one another. Sports teams often have strict roles to play on the field and important role modeling when out of uniform. Men and women in blue have each other's backs. Orchestras hire fiery conductors to ensure the right notes are played at the right time. Few workgroups have such clarity in how they relate to one another.

Rudy's model emphasizes written agreements that can be referred to when problems arise. He advocates beginning with a basic agreement:

- Show up
- Participate fully
- Listen intently
- Tell the truth
- Trust the process
- Honor commitments

Each of these should be discussed and defined. "Show up" means on time and prepared. Other agreements can be added, such as how to resolve disagreements, how to make decisions, and when and how to add and dismiss members.

Everyone on the team must be able to influence how the team operates. Although it is impossible and not useful anyway, influence does not have to be equal. Increased influence can be earned, based on whose influence is most productive for the team. However, influence should not be role-based. Team leaders, for example, may have greater influence than a new member, but only if the influence is productive. A new member may be the team expert in computer software and thus deserve more influence in software issues. The instant a leader attempts to influence the team inappropriately, the team is in trouble.

Influence on the team fosters and clarifies the interdependence necessary for optimal team functioning. One dancer out of step ruins the performance. The same is true of teams. One missed handoff, a misunderstanding, or shared misinformation, and the team falters. There must be a mechanism in place to handle the normal raggedy functioning of people working together. Golfers playing on a team often begin the match with an explicit or implicit blanket apology. "I will try my best," they say to each other, "but I know I will mess up more than once. I don't mean to, but I will, and I promise I will try my best, never give up, and forgive you for any mistakes you make."

It is best if the team itself decides how influencing the team should occur and, as the team does its work, alter any agreements as needed.

4. Personal Reward

According to behavioral psychologists, no one does anything without expecting some benefit. The benefit may be something pleasant, or it may avoid discomfort. Those on a team must be confident that they, as individuals, will derive benefit from their team effort. Sometimes the reward comes from working on the compelling task, the pride of being on the team, or the companionship that arises from working with others. The reward may also include recognition for the team's success, improved chance of personal advancement, or maybe extra hours of paid time off. Whatever it is, the reward must be defined and received.

The more each team member knows of the desired rewards of others, and the more they work toward fulfilling those rewards, the stronger the team.

Of note here is that the change being worked on is usually part of the reward. Recall that many in OD believe change causes negative feelings in employees. This part of teams negates that overblown fear.

Although the eventual outcome may be rewarding, often the way organizations pursue change can create misery. Organizational change includes learning, letting go, and behaving in new ways. This also can include uncertainty, confusion, irritation, and frustration. Even Lean Thinking, famous for its emphasis on reducing waste, often requires hard work to find infinitesimal process improvements. Personal rewards can mitigate these irritants.

The rewards of change can be found in the mutual effort, the discovery of better ways, superior outcomes, fixing what is broken, enhancing what is already good, being thanked, doing something critical, exploring new frontiers, and overcoming obstacles. It isn't hard to find rewards in the change process as long as you know they should be found and provided. Knowing desired rewards and not providing them will obviate future efforts. We humans thrive on rewards, and the more personalized they are, the more rewarding. This does not mean, however, that team rewards are less powerful. If a person is rewarded for team success and views this success as meaningful, a team reward is very satisfying. Being a member of a national or world championship team is the ultimate reward and so is a diamond-studded championship ring. The job of a leader is to know what personal rewards are valued and provide them whenever possible and appropriate.

Rewards should come often, not only at the end of a change. Rewards should not be provided only for success. Effort should be noted and reinforced.

The key to rewards is to keep them meaningful, focus on team rewards, and clearly define what the reward is for. Rewards do not have to be tangible; the best rewards are heartfelt appreciation. The strongest motivators are emotional, not a fistful of dollars. It is fair, useful, and appropriate to ask people what they would like as a reward for change efforts.

Four-Part Teaming Model Summary

The model is symmetrical, but not even. The four parts are numbered in order of importance. The compelling task makes a team necessary and possible. Membership depends on the task and not on who is available. Influence on the team is determined by those on the team including the effective leader. Personal rewards may be identified through the task and the relationship with fellow team members and must be personally meaningful.

If the task itself is not compelling for some members, these participants may feel compelled to be on the team anyway by the importance of their membership, the joy of interacting with others, or in a grand personal reward for team success.

Compared to a workgroup, a high-performing team is dynamic, changing as situations dictate: it endorses team member accountability; the focus is on success often to the point of removing nonperforming team members, and team members are passionate about team efforts and supporting each other.

Building a Team

Building a strong team with the Four-Part Teaming Model is simple. For small teams of less than about twenty people, team-building can take place in one ninety-minute meeting. For larger units, it may take multiple sessions with multiple groups and a few collective meetings to get the job done. The same process as forming smaller teams is followed. Upper limits for team size depends less on the number of members and more on how often and how well they can interact. Rarely, however, can business groups larger than about thirty people form ongoing productive teams, but they may form more productive groups using this model. Large organizations can function well with multiple, small, high-performing teams, not one giant one, again like bicycle wheels and gears.

The only supplies necessary to create a high-performing team the way I do are flip chart paper and a few markers. Gather the people, sit them down, and explain the task at hand. (If the people can define the task, all the better.) Near the top of the first page of the flip chart, write Compelling Task. Along the left side, about eight inches from the edge, list the names of the potential team members as you call on them.

You ask each one "Is the task I explained a compelling task to you? Give it a number from 0 to 10 with 10 being the most important task you could be doing." I have the participants come up to the chart and write their number on the left of their name, while on the right, what about the task led them to choose the number they did. Once everyone has finished, we discuss what we just learned.

If the task is not compelling, we can decide what task would be compelling. If enough people define a compelling task, we continue to the next step. For our example, the task is to reduce the time customers have to wait for service.

```
COMPELLING TASK

10 Joe   Happier
         customers
9 Mary   Like to
         improve
         service
7 Tom    Stronger
         company
```

If you know the potential members, you can list their names on a second sheet labeled Sense of Membership, and as you tell all the members why they were chosen for the team, you write that reason next to the name.

```
SENSE OF MEMBERSHIP

Joe - best IT expert, will en-
sure everything works

Mary - knows policies; we
will avoid legal pitfalls

Tom - creativity; will lead in-
novation efforts
```

Another way of doing it, although riskier, is to have each person come to the flip chart and tell the others why they should be on the team and what they will be accountable to do, which they write next to their name. Make sure this is in enough detail to be meaningful.

At this point, it is useful to discuss if you have the right people for the team and if you need more or fewer, perhaps because some in attendance are not the right people, because the task is not compelling for a few, or their potential contribution is not needed at this time.

On a third sheet labeled Influence on Team, begin listing how the team should work together. Have participants list what they think will work best, understanding this is a living document that will change as needed. Include next steps such as future meetings, work assignments, and measuring progress.

INFLUENCE ON TEAM

Use basic agreement

Use HST for decisions

Meet only when needed

Respect all opinions

On the last sheet, labeled Personal Reward, again list names and ask each person what personal reward they would like for working on the team. Be as specific as possible.

```
┌─────────────────────────────┐
│  PERSONAL REWARD            │
│                             │
│  Joe - extra day off        │
│                             │
│  Mary - more OD training    │
│  on change                  │
│                             │
│  Tom - work on another      │
│  project                    │
│                             │
└─────────────────────────────┘
```

Discuss what has transpired and how this is the beginning of a team effort to work on the compelling task. Answer questions. Hang all four sheets of flip chart paper where team members have access. And there you have it, the formation of a high-performing team.

Sustaining a Team

Sustaining the team is almost as easy as creating it. As often as necessary, not too often and not too infrequently, review the four flip chart pages with the team. Ask a lot of questions. Is the task still compelling? Do we have the right members and are we all contributing as needed? Do we have the resources we need? How well are we working together? How well are we moving toward the goal? How do we make sure we're sustaining the team as well as needed? Are our needs and rewards being met? What do we need to do differently?

Sustaining a team partly depends on the degree and encouragement of diversity. The struggle inherent in accepting and acting upon different points of view strengthens team structure and shows that the group is functioning as a team.

When searching for hurdles, multiple points of view—most notably those of veterans, curmudgeons, negative thinkers, and young upstarts—are invaluable.

Integrating New Members

Rudy Williams suggests using the teaming model to welcome new members. At a team meeting, the team leader should introduce the new member and focus on membership. The leader explains why the new member will make a valuable contribution and then elaborates on why each of the other members is on the team. Telling team stories at this and all the steps enhances the experience.

Team members explain the remaining three team elements. The new member learns how the team makes decisions and how each member influences how the team operates.

Personal rewards are explained, and the new member understands how each member personally benefits from the team effort.

The task is described so the new member understands the importance of the work.

At this point, Rudy suggests discussing any written agreements the team has for working together. Also, discuss any unwritten agreements, such as how and when to consult with each other. It is easier and more productive to go into the details of team functioning after summarizing the four parts rather than when first describing influencing each other.

The result is the new team member is welcomed, informed, integrated, and aware of how to contribute from the beginning. Uncertainty is minimized, and individual and team functioning are maximized.

Teams and Change

Other than these teaming model guidelines, it is best if the team determines how to be a team. The more structure that is imposed, the less the team can be a high-performing team. But remember, all teams have an effective life span. A question to be asked every once in a while is, "Is this still right?"

One of my favorite quotes is not actually a quote. It is an idea, often attributed to military leaders. *If you don't plan, you will fail. If you stick with the plan, you will fail.* For effective organizational development, teams must be formed, and they must change. The power of the team comes from the unity of purpose, and for that team, the purpose makes logical and emotional sense. As long as the purpose makes sense, the team will do whatever it takes, including changing direction and membership, to pursue that purpose. Every employee should be on at least one team, pursuing at least one outcome, and every outcome and method to reach it must make sense. I question if any employee should do any work without being on a team, at least a team of two, which may be just the boss and the employee.

Checklist

High-performing teams are rare and don't emerge just because you want them to. Any effort you make to build teams will be rewarding. Every team will make change easier, more successful, and more sustainable.

As much as I would like to decree using teams and using checklists like the one below, because of the different team methods and models, all I can say with confidence is that teams are superior to workgroups and you're better off to the degree you have them.

Checklist:

1. Every employee in the organization is on a team
2. Every manager can create and sustain teams
3. Teams easily change as needed
4. Emotional rewards are a priority
5. Effort is often rewarded
6. Team rewards are emphasized.

Teams do not exist because a leader says so. They are thoughtfully built from mutual interests into a strong structure that requires regular maintenance. Don't just buy matching hats and call it good.

LEADERS

For sustainable change, leadership is secondary to teams. Leadership is needed pretty much the same way a good butler runs the household: know what needs to be done, make sure it is done, and stay out of the way. A good leader can lead teams, workgroups, lifeboats, congregations, mobs, just about anything. A leader points out a direction and uses whatever influence necessary to enlist people to follow. When gathering followers, the best leaders seem to naturally include many of the elements of a team. These leaders make the upcoming effort compelling and emotionally engage individuals as they join the quest. A good leader doesn't necessarily create a team, but a good team with a good leader is just about invincible.

Anyone with followers is a leader. Any time a leader wants to make a change, followers will do the same—until they don't, sometimes exchanging the old leader for a new one. Kings, queens, despots, emperors, dictators, and those up for re-election have learned this lesson to their disbelief and eventual despair. Leaders who wave the flag in one direction and then march some other way have a problem. Charisma can only go so far; the same is true of force. Making logical and emotional sense of change is a leadership responsibility.

Most leaders and groups of leaders make the same fundamental change error. Behind closed doors, they explore the problem, discuss alternatives, find what they consider the best response, and create talking points to present to employees. This communication package contains an edited history of the issue and preselected details of how the organization will move forward. Early missives often emphasize that little or nothing will change for the workforce. Everyone knows, however, that in the long run, this will not be the case. Employees figure they will be harmed in ways that cannot now be known, but whatever happens, will be awful. Rumors will fly, trust will fly away and so will some employees, out the door or worse for the company, into their shells.

As teams are the thrust, leadership is the guidance system for effective change. Management expert W. Edwards Deming suggested that almost all operational and business problems are the fault of management; we suggest that almost all the problems of change are also the fault of management.

If leadership can better understand what to do and how to do it, organizational change will work better. It will work better if leadership learns how to make logical and emotional sense of change. They think they do now, of course, but they don't.

Trained Leaders Making Sense of Change

Leaders believe that data, facts, logic, good decisions, and thoughtful strategy pave the royal road to success. They believe that emotions should be left outside the door—or at least be suppressed and otherwise minimized while doing company business. Emotions should be avoided when presenting talking points; after all, they are talking points, not emoting points. Change, leadership insists, must be rational. They miss what we mean by change should make sense. Making logical *and* emotional sense must occur with each step of change—even before any change is contemplated.

Leadership Makes Logical Sense of Facts

The keyword to add here is "relevant" facts. Leadership must always tell the truth. However, rarely is the whole truth necessary or helpful. In an ideal world, leadership will first share a clear explanation of current conditions, maybe in the form of a SWOT analysis (Strengths, Weaknesses, Opportunities, and Threats); after all, you hired grown-ups who can handle hearing the truth. This should be done regularly so sharing facts will rarely surprise anyone. At times, leadership will identify a current condition that warrants additional attention, declining revenue, for example. Why this condition needs attention should be explained. Eventually, this condition will be announced as a problem to be solved or an opportunity to be pursued. This is the gap that initiates the possibility of change. That this condition warrants attention should make sense to everyone at this stage before moving to the next.

Leadership, with help sometimes from lower levels, then defines the desired outcome and shares that with everyone. This is discussed (see Communication, below) until it makes sense to everyone.

Leadership shares and gathers opinions about hurdles and concerns. What does the road ahead look like? Robust discussions should ensue. This gathering of employee concerns is where leadership hesitates to venture from their cocoon of facts. Recall how fast the brain moves from problem to solution? Leaders will already know what solutions they prefer and will not want the list of hurdles to derail their favorites. Some leaders with hidden agendas will try to minimize inconvenient hurdles. And it will be difficult for leaders to admit they didn't think of the hurdles identified by lower-level staff. Ensuring that everyone hears about all hurdles is an important element of leadership responsibility to make logical sense of change and to encourage commitment.

The same dynamic plays in listing possible solutions. Leadership knows what it prefers, yet its responsibility to our model demands entertaining other possibilities, openly.

If this making sense of change model is followed, the last step, the chosen path, will make logical sense.

Leadership Makes Sense of Feelings

This is big. Leaders know employees have feelings. At least, they say so. They don't have to like it, and they seem to ignore the fact as much as they can, but leaders live in the real world and should have the help they need to deal with the emotions of workers. Many feelings can arise with the typically fumbled approach to change. They include:

- Sense of loss
- Anger
- Frustration
- Fear
- Sadness
- Guilt
- Helplessness
- Anxiety
- Despair
- Depression

However, to make emotional sense of change and give leaders something positive to focus on, we should concentrate on eliciting these three emotions:

- Inclusion
- Comfort
- Excitement

How do leaders mitigate the long list of negative feelings to change and foster this shortlist of positive emotional reactions? Simple. Use HST to make emotional sense of change. This process automatically and meaningfully verifies the *inclusion* of employees' feelings about the change.

Comfort arises from seeing the change model unfold, understanding why the problem or opportunity requires attention, and understanding why the intended action is the correct action. Comfort will also come from being on a team that is making at least part of the change a reality.

Excitement comes from feeling the problem is solvable, that the goal is the right one and the outcome will be rewarding and well worth the effort. By reducing anxiety and uncertainty and by clear responses to other concerns, a logical sense of change supports the emotional sense of change.

Years ago, I helped a physician-leader put together a presentation about medical errors. As I always do, I asked her how she wanted her audience to be different after her talk. She said she wanted them to more readily admit errors, be more aware of errors while on the job, and help each other cope with and minimize errors. She had a briefcase stuffed with data about medical errors and thus many slides filled with charts and graphs. When I asked her if she had made mistakes, she told me she almost killed a patient. "Why don't you tell that story?" She couldn't do that, she replied. I asked her a week later how the talk went. It was okay, she said, but she was disappointed. We talked more about the intent of her talk and also the almost fatal mistake she made and I wondered out loud again if telling that story would have more impact on her next audience than the data she presented. She told her story the next time. In debriefing that next presentation, she said she almost cried telling about her mistake and that the subsequent discussion by participants couldn't have been better. She learned that feelings, not data, foster involvement and change.

John Kotter suggests the same idea in his book, *The Heart of Change*. Change can make logical and emotional sense only if it includes facts and feelings, not one or the other.

Leaders seem to be afraid of emotions. Business is serious. As perceived by those working upstairs in admin, emotions are a distraction and potential disaster. Yet some emotions are okay: fierce determination is acceptable, as is a passionate commitment. Distrust isn't okay, nor is complacency. Can leaders choose what emotions should be experienced in the workplace? That will not happen. By no longer dodging emotions, leaders can free themselves to elicit the passions that come from working on compelling tasks. Facts *and* feelings are tickets to success.

Making Sense of Leadership

We cannot do justice here to all the demands change puts on leadership. Making logical and emotional sense of change, however, is not that difficult, yet is one area that seems to be a debilitating blind spot to those running the show. There is too much emphasis on executive thinking, dumbing-down issues for the masses and otherwise trying to keep clean and smooth a process that isn't.

The output of high-functional teams and trained leadership is a comprehensive and widespread understanding of the change, productive team interactions, and the broadcast of team successes and failures; this requires effective communication.

Leaders Communicate

Can an organization create policies and procedures to cope with the barrel full of human experiences, thoughts, and emotions that are brought to work each day and also support the changes necessary to stay in business? Similarly, can we expect leaders to become expert psychotherapists, social workers, politicians, seers, and problem solvers? Of course not. Yet organizations must create systems that are solid enough to stay the course and also flexible enough to make changes as needed. We can and must rely on effective communication to sort wheat from chaff, what must stay the same and what can be changed, what is critical and what is common, and advance people from where they are to where they need to be.

If I had to bet, I would wager that most current organizational communication is to inform. Ask anyone why they're holding a meeting and they will say to disseminate information. Most managers haven't quite realized that information itself has no value. Information should be like a protein bar, a source of energy to enable action. But information is often more like a sugary donut, a quick self-indulgence with no nutritional value. Inadequate communication is another leadership contribution to company malnutrition. We communicate information when we should be communicating inspiration. Communication should influence behavior, and a great way of doing that is communicating to stimulate emotions, as the doctor's medical errors presentation did.

When I worked as an internal organizational development consultant, one of my pet peeves was the effort many people made to be professional in their communication. To them, this meant using big words, long and convoluted sentences, multi-page documents, and a somber, serious tone. The same is true with oral presentations: data-filled slides, flat tone, big words, and long sentences. This sugar fix of information generated listeners too bloated and drowsy to move. Yet these managers continued with the same tactic. Being professional was more important than being effective.

The goal of communication is to motivate behavior. For our specific purposes, the goal of communication is to motivate people to work on making changes.

Communication to motivate change efforts must begin with describing the issues that are organizational problems or opportunities. Nothing more will be communicated until employees give feedback that they understand the issue and agree that this issue is important and must be addressed.

For both the issue and the goal, "the medium is the message" (see Marshall McLuhan). If an issue is pressing enough to foreshadow organizational change, it probably should not be introduced through a dry email. Many studies have shown that face-to-face contact is the most effective way to elicit meaningful discussion. Emotionally laden stories are good here (and usually everywhere). The CEO meeting with a few departments is a good idea. Additionally, this initial meeting should include — not just allow — comments. Feedback is critical to learn what message was heard and how it was received. Without feedback to determine impact, broadcast communication may as well be telepathy aimed at the moon. With feedback, a dialogue can begin that enlightens all parties. Thesis, antithesis, and synthesis should continue as long as necessary to get all on board. On board means that employees understand what the issue is and agree that it should be addressed. This may or may not mean change will occur, only that the issue makes logical and emotional sense.

Once everyone is on board with the issue, the same communication effort should be made to define the goal so it makes logical and emotional sense. Again, this does not mean that change is in the wind. At this point, communication is to foster agreement about the importance of the issue and the attractiveness of the goal. To be more engaging, this goal often can be expressed as a compelling vision.

Hurdles and concerns are next. They can be listed first by those in the know (leaders assume this is them) or solicited from employees. However it is done, enough time is taken to ensure everyone has a chance to voice concerns about what it might take to reach the goal, what fears people have and what problems may be encountered. Hurdles should be collected in such a way that everyone can see them. This does not mean that change is in the wind. Nor does it mean change isn't in the wind.

In small organizations, these first three steps can be taken in sequential meetings with the entire staff. This allows time for reflection and peer discussions. With larger companies, this may have to be done in separate groups with findings listed on the company website.

Note that initial communications are not about change. This respects our understanding of the first HST change model essential, taking into account how we humans race from problem to response. Employees must fully understand the issue first. Agreeing to the issue and then the goal is where buy-in occurs. Buy-in does not start at the point of solution implementation. Most change initiatives have it backward, trying to sell a new way before employees have grasped the importance or even the existence of the issue being addressed.

At this point in the HST process, our leadership communication efforts have been to inform employees, in an emotionally compelling way, that the company has an issue that should be addressed. No one is saying change anything. Which is true; maybe the issue can be handled within normal operating procedures, but maybe not. That is our mutual understanding at this point.

It is critical to elicit feedback at each HST step. Either at the end of each step or with every communication effort, employees can be asked how they understand where the company is. In medicine, this is often called "teach back." What did the patient understand concerning the diagnosis and the treatment? By questioning the patient's understanding, the physician can determine the patient's knowledge and level of worry and make necessary corrections. The same concept can be applied to organizational change at each HST step to ensure everyone is on the same page.

Once employees accept that there is an issue to address, that the goal is important and makes logical and emotional sense, and that the leaders and employees have a good understanding of what hurdles might be encountered, possible approaches can be identified. Still, no change is mandated even at this stage. We're only looking at options.

When organizations communicate change in the form of, "We will do X, Y, and Z," resistance is a natural response. When we make sense of change, when we investigate and communicate issues first, we engage employees, we don't manhandle them, and we don't need to persuade them. And so far in our HST communication effort, we have not raised the specter of impending change, only the importance of an issue and the appeal of the goal. We have also communicated our global understanding of the ramifications of the issue. Rather than creating resistance, the HST change model mobilizes employee participation.

The next step of communicating is listing solution possibilities. The first solution that can always be listed is "don't change anything." If the consequences of doing nothing appear dire, employees will accept that change is now in the wind and that is okay.

The last step is to decide what actions to take from the listed options. This too should be as open a process as possible no matter how decisions are made.

Once a course of action is decided upon, communication must monitor how the change is going, who is affected, what goals are reached, what isn't working well and what is being done about it. As much as possible, these should be face-to-face reports with plenty of discussion time.

This is when leadership communication is critical for sustaining change and, in fact, of sustaining a successful business. It is by clearly communicating how a change is working or not working that the best organizations shine, and trust is maintained. A company sabotages change efforts when it fears failure, punishes those who make mistakes, and buries bad news.

If taking a chance is a dumb move in a company, change is a hollow endeavor. Communicating errors and bad results keeps open the door to improvement.

Communication is a challenge for leaders because most of them have been communicating since they were babies. They think they have the hang of it when they don't. Communication should:

- Be simple and direct
- Most often be face-to-face
- Be to motivate behavior
- Include feedback
- Include stories

True communication, meaning communicating the good and the bad, may leave leaders feeling naked to the world, but leaders feeling naked is a reasonable price to pay for success.

Leaders Solve Problems

Over forty years ago I was a young, eager, innocent psychologist at a guidance clinic staffed with veteran social workers. At our two-hour weekly staff meetings, discussions about a problem might take an hour or more before we came to a resolution. It drove me crazy when I offered a solution within the first few minutes that was eventually agreed to an hour later. I took aside a senior social worker one afternoon and asked her why it took so long to agree. She said, "It takes time for a group to process." I didn't know what this meant but thought it must mean something useful. It wasn't until a few years later I realized that this "processing" was incompetent problem-solving.

There is no end to human cognitive foibles. We would rather give up a prize for ourselves if by doing so we deprive someone we don't like from profiting. And as learned from moral dilemma studies, we would kill an innocent stranger to save multiple other lives, but only if we didn't have to touch the person (like pushing them off a bridge).

Here are a few observations of what we're like:

- We respond like Pavlov's dogs to variable ratio reinforcement schedules (think slot machines).
- We think the best of our friends and the worst of our enemies, and we mistrust those who are unlike us.
- Sometimes the best ideas are laughed at.
- Often, a group of independent average people can solve a problem better than an expert.
- We vote on solutions as if voting somehow identifies the best one.
- Rarely do we define the best answer so we know it is the best answer.

- Some leaders (gasp) make decisions to protect their turf.

How do we overcome these everyday realities that lead to bad, reflexive, political, power-driven, secretive, etc., etc., problem-solving?

The answer is to make the problem-solving process transparent, make it measurable, and ensure it makes logical and emotional sense to all participants. Effective problem-solving supports teamwork and leadership by identifying a compelling task leading to a compelling goal. Effective problem solving also establishes a supportive environment that allows candor and chance-taking and fosters communication through an abundance of feedback loops. Leaders keep teammates on task when their brains naturally race to instant solutions. Teamwork fosters the peer commitment and accountability required by comprehensive problem-solving.

Sit in a corner of a meeting room and observe the action. You'll see a discussion or a debate, often with no one recording the ideas. It will consist of people talking until someone says, "I think we have talked this to death, let's take a vote." Squint so you can see the details. If the vote is verbal, you'll notice some participants not saying anything. If the vote is by raising hands, some hands will shoot up, while others barely make it above table height. Both actions suggest less than optimal participation or buy-in.

This tepid enthusiasm is not always about the outcome but is often about decision-making. Somehow, despite all the time spent on the discussion, one or more participants were not meaningfully involved.

Problem-Solving the HST Way

Imagine an extended family dinner in greater Los Angeles: ten adults sitting around a table enjoying each other's company. Suddenly, one says, "I have an idea. Why don't we go on a family vacation?"

Immediately someone answers, "Great idea and I know the perfect place, San Francisco. It has everything for a great time, Fisherman's Wharf, Chinatown, streetcars…"

"Hold on," comes another voice. "When I go on vacation I want to relax in the sun, lying next to a pool. Palm Springs is where we have to go."

"Hey," arises a third voice. "If you want sun and water, San Diego has great beaches and the entire Pacific Ocean. If we're going anywhere, we have to go to San Diego."

Thus the debate begins. Before the main meal is finished, someone mercifully ends the point-counterpoint by suggesting a vote. All agree that whatever place gets the most votes wins. The tally is San Francisco four votes, Palm Springs three votes, and San Diego three votes. San Francisco wins.

But how logically and emotionally sensible would it be to go to San Francisco? Four people wanted to go while six did not. Let's say they, like many groups before them, eliminate one option to make the decision more definitive. A renewed debate, more heated this time with the San Francisco and San Diego people attacking Palm Springs, which leads to the Palm Springs trio opting out. A new vote results in a five-five tie. Should a coin flip determine the locale of the family vacation? No. They agreed on this anyway. They debate through dessert and then vote again. This time San Francisco wins, seven to three. And so San Francisco becomes their destination. If they were honest, they would admit that only four wanted to go; the rest gave in out of fatigue, mounting disinterest, or the realization they were not affecting the decision.

This kind of outcome is pervasive in organizational development. People discuss solutions, debate them, and often decide only because they are out of time. Leaders must lead problem-solving better than they currently do.

For problem-solving, we have HST, a tool to make the process transparent, measurable, and credible to all participants. Let's restart the family dinner. Appetizers have just been served. Suddenly, one says, "I have an idea. Why don't we go on a family vacation?"

Immediately a second mature and thoughtful voice adds, "That sounds like a solution. What's the issue?"

"Oh yeah, you have that issue/goal gap thing going. How's this? Our family has great family dinners. There is probably something we can do together that would be even better."

"Okay. The opportunity is for all of us to have even better quality time together. Do I have that right?" Everyone holds thumbs up for a visual measure of approval. "Who wants to define the goal?"

"I will," says another voice. "Our goal is greater quality time together that includes the whole family, and everyone has a great time and wants to do it again or even something grander."

"Sounds good to me. Everyone agree?" Another show of thumbs, all pointing up.

"How about hurdles and concerns? I've written the opportunity and goal and can keep a list as you yell them out."

"If we go somewhere, it has to be someplace warm and sunny."

"I want to swim."

"I want to eat great food."

"I want a lot of different kinds of food."

"I want to relax by a pool."

"I want to do exciting things."

"How about learning things?"

"Can't take too much time. I have a lot of work to do."

"I have to afford it. No more than $900."

The family compiled a list of twenty-two hurdles and concerns; many were must-haves. By this time, they were eating the main meal.

"All right. Possible solutions?"

"Go to San Francisco."

"Palm Springs."

"San Diego."

"A cruise."

"Stay at home and go on day trips."

"Take a class together."

They listed about fifteen options. They then compared the possible solutions to the hurdles and the defined goal. The decision was easy, a cruise to Ensenada and back, including everyone learning how to play Texas hold 'em poker.

The process was transparent. It was obvious what part of problem-solving was being worked on, and notes were taken for easy review. Everyone took part, knowing what and when to contribute, and all agreed when each step was completed.

Assembling the solution with five steps, rather than debating it until exhaustion set in, made logical and emotional sense to all. Dessert included an animated discussion of the fun they would have.

The Real World

In the real world, issues are complex and often hard to parse out of the flurry of challenges that face decision-makers. Problem-solving isn't easy, but it can be easier and more efficient and effective.

We have not yet evolved as a species to read one another's minds, and unless we slow our discussions, make them transparent, take them in measurable steps and record them for all to see, we are operating almost at the level of chattering monkeys.

Although the five steps make up the core of the organizational HST change model, they can be applied every time problems arise in implementing or sustaining change — from what room to use for a meeting to how much should be spent to acquire a rival business.

What should be in place for change problem-solving is listed on the next page:

- The organization has a standard, transparent way to solve problems.
- Everyone participates meaningfully in identifying problems and opportunities.
- No one is surprised by the intended organizational changes.
- Secret negotiations are rare or absent.
- Decisions make logical and emotional sense.

When a change from the top is offered in visible steps that are matched with how the employees think and feel, the sense of ownership and engagement can increase, and commitment will trump compliance.

A standardized problem-solving process defines goals, roles, and procedures so errors are handled productively and immediately. When we take steps together, we're all responsible for the results.

All actions should be public knowledge, put up on a board somewhere or on the company web pages. They should be discussed regularly. And always ask, "How will we know?" to make sure all concerns are addressed.

Leaders Ensure Knowledge Exchange

If done poorly, gaining and sharing knowledge can impede

change processes. Knowledge for our purposes is knowledge about the change process, what must happen to make change successful, what the change may mean, whether the change is successful or not and what to do about it, what role individuals and teams play in the change effort, and what abilities individuals and teams must have and use for success.

The first of our knowledge priorities, of course, is to ensure that the change makes logical and emotional sense. This is not automatic when the issue is first identified. It often takes executive leadership many months to understand the exigencies of the marketplace. How is the average worker to comprehend the grand scheme of things when given only corporate talking points? Here are a few questions to answer: Why is this important now? Why is this important to our company? Why is this important to employees? Knowledge about change begins with the first step, identifying the issues that may eventually require change.

Knowledge About Change

In the best organizations, change is a constant. Change happens all the time, in all areas, and is expected as part of the work. In most organizations, change is sudden, often unexpected, is in response to serious threats, and causes distress among employees. This is where core knowledge about change is a significant strength. Unfortunately, the knowledge most employees carry with them is that change benefits the organization, often at significant cost to employees. The basic knowledge everyone should have of change is that except in case of emergencies, the need for change will make logical and emotional sense to all concerned before any change is made. If change is made without general prior knowledge, it will be explained using HST as soon as possible, and the change will then make sense. Trust grows when knowledge flows.

What Must Happen to Make Change Successful

The change must solve an identified problem or exploit an opportunity. A change will not be successful if it is a pet project of the board chair (or president, vice president, department manager or supervisor), the latest corporate fad, imitates a rival or any other mindless reaction that doesn't have an antecedent reason for the organization to sit up and pay attention. Change must be meaningfully connected to something employees feel is important.

What the Change May Mean

Few people board a ship without knowing where and when landfall will be, and without believing that the arrival will be a good thing, maybe at a sunny place with palm trees. The same should be true for any change. Leaders must ensure knowledge of a change includes gains for employees. A stronger company may be an exciting outcome for the execs, but employees would prefer that the outcome benefits their jobs.

One nice outcome would be documentation that the change will increase job security—a rare instance in which data may have a greater impact than stories.

A huge boost to knowledge is to include in the meaning of change the potential negative or unintended consequences. People often like to hear the bad news first, assuming that the good news will cancel out the bad. This is true with change efforts. What might happen if the change fails? Leaders should answer this question early and keep answering other fears as they arise. This is a delicate element of change and a test of leadership. How do you always tell the truth, but not always be telling it? Frequently success depends on optimism leading to dedication, not reality leading to hopelessness. However, effort is often highest when the chances of success are only fifty-fifty and less enthusiastic when the chances are much better. Share everything you can and ask for feedback.

Individual Roles in the Change Effort

Which brings us to change knowledge and individual roles in the change effort. As you know, those affected by the change should be involved in the change effort. But what kind of knowledge must they have?

Every employee affected by a possible change should be involved in identifying the issue. This does not mean any of them must have ideas of how to respond to the issue. The old saw "don't come to me with a problem unless you have a solution in mind" is ridiculous. People can identify a problem, but not know how to solve it. You want to know about problems as soon as possible. This problem-plus-solution expectation puts up a needless barrier to knowledge and communication. Additionally, if someone must come up with a solution, it may not be the best one and you end up disparaging their solution and backing up to focus on defining the issue better anyway.

Employees should contribute their knowledge about the change in all the ways they can, which is part of their sense of membership and influence on the team. Each employee who contributes should feel that her contribution is necessary for success, even if that contribution is solely to find hurdles. Find the department naysayer, enlist her to identify hurdles and you will multiply your chances of success.

Abilities Employees Must Have for Success

Any and every employee can contribute to any and every organizational change. From the dullest to the smartest, from the most creative to the thickest concrete head, and from the most engaged to the most sullen, everyone should be included in the change. We can borrow from Karl Marx (and others) to know what to do: "From each according to his ability, to each according to his needs." This means that we should enable everyone to contribute whatever they can and reward them in meaningful ways for their contribution.

"According to his ability" also means that no one is left out. A concrete head, for example, who doesn't seem to understand new ideas, can be useful to edit or clarify complicated messages. A high-flying creative type can be brought back to earth by someone with a sullen attitude. The executive can list profound ideas, one of which resonates with the janitor and the idea is then promoted from the bottom up. There is no end to the wisdom of a group of people; to prima facie exclude anyone is usually a mistake. Enhance the change by growing together in the effort. Attack the problem with gusto and goodwill to all. Learn together from your collective mistakes. Change is made more difficult by trying to over-control it. Change is untidy if you do it right, and you are doing it right when everyone's wisdom is sought and included.

The Role of Mistakes in Change

Just as falling when learning to ski is part of improving, making errors in change efforts can be a good thing. Change must prove its value, and that can be judged only after it is tried. Learning by trial and error in small steps strengthens a change effort. Hits and misses should be broadcast to the entire organization without the shame of the blame game.

It should be clear to everyone in the organization that the effect of any change is uncertain. As many safeguards will be applied, as much foresight used as humanly possible, and every risk identified before a change is implemented. Most errors and mistakes will be human ones, not of the new methods and processes. Practicing before implementation will be the rule. Discovering errors and omissions will be celebrated as necessary steps toward mastery. Lessons learned will be lessons applied.

The more mistakes are accepted, the grander the leaps that can be made. When risks are great, take small steps. When risks are minimal, reach for the moon. Encourage everyone's Einstein, MacGyver, and Edison. As people learn and are allowed to extend themselves, they will stretch themselves, learn more, and accomplish more.

With change efforts, sharing knowledge is critical. Imagine the benefit when a failed change effort in one department is shared with another. The other department uses lessons learned to succeed in a similar effort, shares its new knowledge enabling the first one to try again and succeed. Long-term, shared errors may be the most useful knowledge for continued learning and development.

Leadership by the Right Objective

With the HST change model, our first objective is employee inclusion; our second is improving the business. You can do both. You should do both. You should do them in that order.

Good leadership requires good followership. The more a leader enables people to follow, by making the goal and the path to the goal make sense, the more successful the leader will be.

Poor leaders or an authoritarian goal-obsessed culture make team building nearly impossible. For survival, individuals form cliques that become self-serving and can be anti-organization. Trained leaders create teams, provide guidance, direction, and support, and do so transparently.

Leaders should also know change often includes altering how people work together. Unless people interactions, skill development, process handoffs, and the like are included in change effort assessments, these downstream consequences can create confusion, leading to resentments and irritation. If leaders declare that enhancing individuals, people interactions, and teams are critically important, change will work.

How many times have you heard business leaders say, "People are our most important asset" or similar pronouncements? Sadly, you have probably heard the statement more than you have seen the idea in action. Had that grandiose proclamation been true, leads, supervisors, and managers would be promoted for their managerial skills as opposed to meeting production goals or other outcome measures. Leads would receive six months of leadership training, supervisors would be provided a year's training and mentoring, and managers would join together for two years of collaborative training and mentoring. But they don't receive anything near that.

Instead, these exemplars of the Peter Principle cling to leadership roles with over-control, micromanagement, secrecy, suppression, blindness, hope, and denial. Trouble is, this cascade of incompetence flows from the top down. No one in this line of leadership can help those below; few in this line seem to appreciate the harm being done.

Everyday Leadership

As with mac & cheese, Legos, and the blues, you can do a lot with the HST model because it is simple. As any decent patriarch would, I used the Four-Part Teaming model to help my granddaughter join the family team at a point in her life when she liked to dart through parking lots. I told her everyone in the family was on the team and asked her if she wanted to be on the team too. When she said yes, I told her everyone in the family had jobs equal to how old they were. I asked her how old she was. "Three." "Then," I said, "you have three jobs. Want to know what they are?" She nodded yes. "Your first job is to have fun." She liked that. "Your second job is to learn things." She liked that one too. "Your third job is to be safe." That one wasn't so good. "But you know what?" I asked. "What?" "I have the same job you have, to keep you safe. We have the same job!" She thought that was great and from then on held my hand in parking lots because we were on the same team working on the same job.

Trained Leader Checklist

From families to foundations, from clubs to corporations, people who lead people should do so transparently, with supreme communication skills and the interest and ability to meaningfully include others in every change effort.

Checklist:

1. Leaders lead high-performing teams
2. Employees are treated like people
3. Leaders tell emotionally engaging stories
4. Leaders operate from well-known universal values
5. Leaders make logical and emotional sense of change
6. Knowledge of what works and doesn't work is emphasized and shared
7. The HST model for change is common knowledge
8. Managers are accountable to engage employees
9. Managers sustain employee engagement
10. Everyone's role in change is understood
11. Mistakes are made into positives
12. Change provides benefits to everyone
13. Leaders lead from the middle, not way out in front

The list is long; leaders have a lot of responsibility. But it's doable. It can be fun and rewarding at the top.

OUT FOR A SPIN

HOW HST IS APPLIED

Pacific Coast Medical is a fictitious organization representing many of the characteristics of a successful business. PCM is medium-large, with a six-hundred-million-dollar budget and four thousand employees spread over eleven sites. Services include primary care, specialty care, and outpatient surgery with affiliations with the major hospitals in the area. It has been in business for over seventy years and has a good reputation in the community but is suffering from stagnant growth, Medicare payment reductions, squeezing by insurance carriers, increasing costs from suppliers, growing competition from larger providers, higher expectations of patients, and an aging staff.

On a trip home over Thanksgiving, family practice doctor and clinic director Steve Hull was intrigued by the ticket kiosks he came across at the airport check-in. We could do that at each of our clinics, he thought. In prior years, he would have taken his idea to the director of clinics, who would have taken it to the board. The board would look into the feasibility and decide what to do. However, Dr. Hull was well trained in organizational development and knew what he had on his hands, a solution looking for a problem.

All the time, in the dark of night or bright light of day, somewhere, someone in leadership returns from a conference with a great new idea. This is a fundamental change error, trying to attach a shiny new trinket onto a well-oiled, fast-moving chain. Most often, this means the people who do the work are told to try this new way to fix a problem that either doesn't exist or is a minor problem that should be addressed after more important ones have been fixed. Dr. Hull was aware of this type of mistake.

Identifying the Issue/Opportunity

The old way was not a good way to initiate change at the new PCM. Dr. Hull had created an HST template he wanted to try, and his great idea of using kiosks for medical check-in was his first opportunity.

The template was a tool to make sure he did not make the classic error of promoting his solution instead of taking the time to understand the relevant issue(s). It was for him to manage the initial set-up for possible change. His first template he called, "HST Start" and is presented on the next page.

HST Step	Thoughts
Issue	PCM reception has the opportunity to improve services
Goal	To determine if a gap exists between the current level of services and possible future services and define what that gap is
Hurdles	Little knowledge of current services/limitations Don't know the pros and cons of medical kiosks Easy to leap to making a case for kiosks
Possible solutions	Create a guiding coalition Discover pros/cons of general kiosks Identify reception issues via reception manager Question users of medical kiosks
Choose solution	Identify reception issues via managers as the first step
Notes	Want to try out kiosks Focus on reception needs and involvement Use this opportunity to help train others in organizational change

Notice that Dr. Hull, enamored with the kiosk idea as he was, did not focus on the kiosk idea but on two important change dynamics, that receptionists' needs should be the focus and that they should be included in every step of the process. Any sign at the start that he wanted to try adding kiosks to reception processes would sabotage the improvement effort. He asked Sue, the lead receptionist, to identify the issues the receptionists most wanted to address. By email, she asked the seven receptionists, "What check-in problems should we put on a fix-it list?" and received fourteen different issues, with three being mentioned most. These were:

- When the line is long people have to wait to check in
- When someone's check-in takes a long time and quick intakes have to wait behind them
- Check-in process moves among too many computer screens, which is slow and frustrating

Dr. Hull wondered if other clinic sites had similar issues. Since reception representatives met monthly, he asked this group to compile a list of reception issues too. When their list was similar, he knew he had a textbook opportunity for organizational development.

Again, using email, he polled all the receptionists to ask, "Would you be willing to investigate and perhaps improve the long line problem and the uneven needs of patients when they are waiting to check in?" They all agreed and defined an issue that made logical and emotional sense:

> Issue: there is an undefined gap between current
> check-in and optimal check-in.

Next, he formed a team of his local receptionists and informed the other sites they would be involved as consultants along the way. He made sure everyone on the team considered this work compelling. Then he enjoyed telling each potential member why they were needed on the team. Each nodded and smiled at his encouraging comments and looked at each other when he described the others. The feeling in the room was of mutual appreciation and optimism.

Discussing how to work together and identifying personal rewards completed the initial team-building. He would lead the effort with Sue's help once the team approved his guiding the effort and his ability to be the right team leader.

Every team activity, he told the local reception team, would be shared with all the receptionists and the other clinic directors for their input. He made sure everyone knew that their contribution every step of the way was critical.

Defining the Goal

The next step according to HST was to define the goal. He went to his local team to determine what the goal would be and then shared that with everyone else before moving forward. They met in two groups because of scheduling realities. It took two meetings of each group and a bit of wordsmithing:

> The goal: no patients will wait over four minutes to be checked in, and no patients will have to wait over two minutes if they have a simple check-in.

This goal, all the receptionists agreed, might be impossible to reach, but if they did, it would be immensely satisfying for them and the patients. They faced an imposing task. Often, the line could consist of ten patients or more, even when all five reception stations were open. And how to identify someone waiting in line as a likely quick check-in was anyone's guess. Maybe some kind of triage system like in an emergency room might work, but all were cautioned not to race to any solutions.

This goal, with a gap more assumed than measured at this point, was sent to the larger PCM reception team for review and was also sent to PCM leadership. Feedback from both groups was positive, and the goal remained the same as the local group had defined. They felt good about everyone agreeing with them and were eager to figure out what improvements to make.

Listing Hurdles and Concerns

Next, again by email, Dr. Hull asked the local team to list hurdles and for the PCM reception team to do the same. Dr. Hull shared both lists with the local reception team, the PCM reception team, and the leadership team.

Here are the first ten from their combined list:

1. Solution should work at all sites
2. Varied demands for check-in during the day
3. Can't hire more receptionists
4. No receptionists will lose their job, no matter what the solution
5. Cost should be minimal (to be defined later)
6. Solution should be in place within two weeks of the decision
7. Solution should be long term, not a Band-Aid
8. Learning new skills should be minimized
9. Patients must like the new process
10. Solution must work in concert with all down-stream processes

This list was sent to all involved with the declaration that these were the primary hurdles/concerns that would be used to evaluate the possible solutions, with the remaining ones used as tie-breakers as needed. All agreed that this was a reasonable and practical approach.

At this point, he noted that specific personal rewards had not been provided to date. He mentioned that to Sue, who promised to follow up with the reception team. Most had said all they wanted was a better process and insisted that was enough. Two said they wanted to learn the change process better and were confident they would learn simply by doing this work. Sue said that she would think of something additional they all could enjoy.

Listing Solutions

Dr. Hull then asked the reception team to list all the solutions they could think of. He instructed them not to be bound by any of the hurdles—anything they could come up with would be fine—and he also suggested they meet in small groups to brainstorm as frequently as possible. "No idea is a bad idea, and the more ideas the better," he told them. These were the receptionists' first ten:

1. Create two lines, one for simple check-ins, the other for those with greater needs
2. Check in via smartphones somehow
3. Kiosk like at the airport (!)
4. Check in according to appointment times
5. Two lines, one for appointment check-in, the other for walk-in clinic visits
6. Lines sorted by alphabetical order
7. Have rover receptionist with a tablet who will go to the line and identify and do the fast check-ins
8. Check people in while they sit in the waiting room
9. Create an online pre-check-in system
10. Eliminate front desk check-in and have MA do it in the exam room

The last one, eliminating the check-in process, was courageous, and was maybe submitted because it sounded good, but would be next to impossible to implement. Dr. Hull was pleased to see the kiosk idea come up. If no one had mentioned it, he would have had to make sure it was one of the possible solutions to consider. After all, he was on the team too. But he would have to make sure his idea didn't receive extra consideration. Everyone being equal would be a good lesson for all.

Choosing the Best Solution

Again because of scheduling problems, the local reception team met in two groups to decide what change or changes to make. They ended up meeting twice and then formed a subgroup to make the final decision. They kept the larger reception team aware of their thoughts. To Dr. Hull's chagrin and yet to his enlightenment, the reception team chose separate lines. The kiosk idea was fairly considered and rejected for the time being.

Part of the effort included collecting data on the wait times in line. The receptionists spent a week collecting the wait time of the last person in line four times an hour for three hours in the morning and three hours in the afternoon. With that data, they could assess the change. The new way would begin next week.

IMPLEMENTING THE CHANGE

Changing is an unhappy experience if it doesn't work. "Work" means things are better in a significant way. That's the promise, the challenge, and the obligation. Although disappointed his kiosk idea did not make the cut, Dr. Hull still wanted to spearhead the effort to improve the patient's reception experience. As the one with the most organizational development experience, he was confident he could avoid common pitfalls and ensure employees had a positive experience and a positive outcome. To do that, he created another checklist:

Reception Line Implementation Checklist

Action	Goal	Done by
Keep the local team active in implementation and the other teams informed	A core of change agents is created	10/9

Ensure the local team uses HST when encountering problems	Users are skilled in HST	10/10
Include executive leadership in progress reports and ask PCM reception group to plan how to use the local group's experience at other sites	Leadership actively supports the change effort	10/10
Create visual controls of the change and a change-feedback loop for patients and the other teams	Progress can be measured Interest in sustaining is high	10/10
Provide the reward Sue wanted to give	Staff rewarded for their effort	10/18
As information is gained, have local reception team create progress and learning reports for others in PCM	Everyone at PCM informed and other groups are considering changes	10/24

Dr. Hull suggested that the receptionists post the new process data on the wall behind them for all to see, including patients.

"Don't put up numbers," he advised. "Create a colorful graph that will tell you in an instant if things are improving or not." He smiled. "This is a learning experience for all of us."

So they did. After designing a two-line check-in system, they posted information for patients so they could choose the correct line, informed them personally of the new process at check-in, and posted wait times each day on the line graph behind them. Steadily, the wait time in the check-in line was reduced. After three weeks, it hit their wait time goals. With this success, they invited the receptionists from other sites to visit and see for themselves what the new system offered. Within two weeks all the other sites had the two-line system in operation and began collecting data about their wait times to create a new standard. An added item for the monthly reception meeting was to compare the wait times at each site. There were lessons to learn and share from the longest and the shortest wait times. The larger group also thought about creating in-the-moment quality measures. How did patients feel about that particular check-in experience? Thus, a change was made, and a painless continuous improvement effort was born. The change made logical and emotional sense.

BRINGING IT HOME

WHAT'S NEW?

How we improve our change management should itself follow our new change model. We should change nothing until we identify current organizational development weaknesses and opportunities (the issues). Improving the way we improve must make logical and emotional sense.

The HST model improves how the human brain naturally processes information and makes decisions. The model also emphasizes the benefit of visual control to externalize problem-solving so participants understand the process and effectively contribute. The model stresses the importance of both logical and emotional information exchange to solidify the value of the change, the acceptance of change, and its implementation and sustainability.

The HST model focuses on the needs and functioning of people. Thus, the model is built on the externalization of brain activities and the reliance on two organizational elements, teams and leaders, to power and support people needs. Each HST step can be measured and revised as needed along the way, further supporting expanded participation. A major strength is transparency and inclusion. Another strength is the logical sequence. Yet another strength is using this model to identify and support emotional needs and expectations.

Assessing the New Model

Current organizational change models focus on business management structures. They assume that change is a given and seek to define leadership and worker roles to achieve positive business outcomes. They also assume employees must be cajoled to support change efforts. The HST model begins with biology and ends with organizational development, expanding from the individual brain to the collective wisdom of the individuals who make up an organization, ensuring everyone participates in the right ways at the right times. Other models entice employees to climb aboard the change train and work to keep them in their seats. HST asks employees if they're interested in laying track, building a locomotive, designing the cars, and choosing speed and destination. Users of the HST model can encase it in any other change model they wish or use it as a standalone method.

Another factor that characterizes this model is it should not be applied as a formula. Every organization must grow into its own version of HST designing together what works best. Build it, together, with the needs, resources, and interests you already have so it works for your circumstances. This means that processes will not change according to a mandated approach or predetermined solutions, but participants will discover together, through problem-solving, how to improve. It will be scrappy, mistakes will be made, but change will come. People will smile, they will be engaged, they will seek opportunities and make good things happen. Invitation rather than mandate, transparency of mental and emotional processes, defined and measured steps, and mutual investment and accountability make the difference.

Changing Change

Not much beats learning a new skill, trying it out, finding success, and everyone shaking your hand and singing your praises. Let's see if we can make this happen where you work. Remember, when you make any organizational change, you must first pinpoint the issue and the goal, and then the change will sell itself.

The question to ask at your business is: "Are we making all the improvements we should and are we doing it as well as we can?" The answer should always be no. Next, find out why your organization is not making all the improvements it should, or as well as it could. You'll find that people say there isn't enough time, there aren't enough resources, we're too busy with more important projects, etc. So next ask: "Do we need to get better at how we improve?" Once you've collected all the answers, you'll have a beginning idea of the gap between your current organizational development and where you could be. Next, do appreciative inquiry. Ask about possibilities with questions such as: "What can we become? What expectations of ourselves should we have? Where can we be in two years?" Then ask: "What do we have to do to get there? What do we want to do to get there?" You're creating a list of problems and opportunities that will make logical and emotional sense. Spread the word; set up a checklist of problems and opportunities. Get everyone involved. Once people agree that things should and can be better, you can improve change where you work.

Be a Team Advocate

As you compile a list of problems and opportunities, begin creating high-performing teams wherever you can. This might be your biggest challenge. Most employees have not experienced the benefits of being on a team and don't have a good understanding of what a real team is like. They might be called a team, but they've likely bought into leadership cheerleading, "Rah-rah, we're a team, our people are really something." With your workgroup and perhaps with one or two others, use what you know about team-building to build real teams. Naturally, you don't create teams without a purpose. Identify the gap between the value of workgroups and the value of teams. Discuss this gap, explore options, do an appreciative inquiry about teams; make logical and emotional sense about team-building. Look at what you currently accomplish and see if the team wants to do more. You could create a vision statement that is engaging and is doable through a compelling task.

If you want to use Rudy Williams' Four Part Teaming Model, you could:

1. Use making logical and emotional sense of improving organizational change as the compelling task.
2. Make sure everyone on the team knows why they are needed on the team and their accountabilities.
3. Discuss, write out, and post the rules and expectations of how the team will work together.
4. Discuss personal rewards and post the list for all to see.
5. Make sure interdependencies are defined and accepted.
6. Use HST with problems and opportunities.
7. Widely communicate successes and failures.

When the team is created, it should meet often enough to monitor the work on the compelling task, how successful it is, and what isn't working.

Involve Leadership

Leadership must know HST and be able to use this model in just about every situation. Just as Dr. Hull did not use his position of authority to push his agenda, leaders must be able to monitor and motivate without unduly influencing the change process. The worst action leaders can take is to encourage employees to use HST to find good solutions and then abort what employees have discovered to implement actions the leaders prefer while thanking the employees for their effort.

HST must be transparent. This has the effect of keeping leaders forthright, but it also promotes employee support as they find better ways of getting the work done.

An important challenge for leadership is to accept that change is untidy, and mistakes will be made. Although HST is transparent, it can be manipulated and land on a less than optimal solution. Employees can also become frustrated at the perceived extra work of finding solutions when they're used to debating solutions from the start (ones waiting in their hip pockets). Leaders must be aware of the effort necessary to implement change through HST and provide support until this model can be ingrained in the organization's change practices.

The majority of stress from using HST is spending time and energy to fully understand and agree to issues and goals, and not racing to solutions. This is contrary to how the mind wants to work and why the method is called Harnessing the Speed of Thought.

Communicate, Communicate, Communicate

As we've mentioned, communication includes feedback. Most organizations are bad at feedback systems and usually, feedback is negative. As you implement the new change model, define all feedback as useful: *feedback is a productive and necessary clarifier for a message or results of our efforts*. Emphasize feedback as the most important element of communication.

Solve Every Problem, Resolve Every Conflict

Current change models address the universal problem of conflict. Some organizational change experts focus on the conflict of company politics and culture while others see conflicts arising as natural resistance to change.

Using HST you will find that most conflicts are caused by individuals or groups being unaware they are defining issues and goals differently and only seem to be in conflict over what solutions to implement. They are arguing about step four or five when they should pay attention to differences in steps one and two. Once everyone is on the same step, conflicts either disappear or differences actually help refine the steps.

Engage Engagement

Many OD approaches are concerned with the difference between compliance and commitment. You can force employees to act in predetermined ways, or you can enable them to act in their and the organization's best interests. Melding the employee's personal mission to that of the company works very well. This means understanding what the employee wants out of the job. Is it money, status, security, growth, enjoyment, friendships? Employees have personal missions, whether or not they are aware of them. Find out what the mission is; discuss how to fulfill the personal mission while the employee contributes to the company mission. If a mutual issue for the employee and the company is how to combine the two missions, and the mutual goal is that both missions will be fulfilled, you have engagement.

This approach also can be applied to work-teams. Make sure the compelling task of the team and the mission of the company are compatible and that the team knows of how much their efforts are contributing to the welfare of the company and all other employees. This sense of belonging to the larger group is invaluable.

Enhance the Payoff

Should employees have a stake in the company? If the best work is done when employees own the process and the outcome, doesn't it make sense they will do even better when they own a piece of the action? Research says, "yes."

I've worked in places where candy bars were given out as rewards. I enjoyed them but thought it was feeble management thinking that this was an effective way to reward grown-ups. One Thanksgiving we were all given turkeys. This was nice too but did nothing to increase my motivation for work. Don't fall into the trap of tangible rewards; the real action is in meaning. We've been pushing that change should make logical and emotional sense. Rewards should fit the same criteria.

A logical reward is one that is proportionate to the effort or result and is often associated with the benefit to the organization.

For example, if an effort saves the company ten million dollars, a monetary reward makes logical sense. A few days off is less logical, but still appropriate. A certificate of appreciation is less so.

However, a certificate of appreciation could make sense as an emotional reward. Say an employee gave CPR to a stricken coworker. A ceremony, a certificate of appreciation, and dinner with the CEO might make perfect emotional sense as a reward.

No reward is better than the wrong reward. The wrong reward is ignorant, insulting, and dismissive. When employees realize that it works to be honest, this is when good communication and feedback can enhance the effect of rewards. Ask the one who deserves the reward, "How can we best show our appreciation for what you have done?" and do what you're told whenever you can. At first, you may be told what is culturally correct, but as everyone learns honesty is expected, you will hear what people truly want.

Share the Knowledge

Many people feel more is learned in college dorms than in classrooms. Employees sharing ideas and experiences, telling stories, and laughing together, build knowledge in the most productive ways. In the typical office, the water cooler is a fountain of wisdom compared to the normal department meeting. Often, official channels for communication are the least helpful.

Trainers know of the quick decay of lessons learned in formal classes. By bedtime after a daylong session, most of what was taught is already lost. What you hear is quickly gone. What you observe is retained longer while what you do sticks better. What you discuss, reflect on, and do sticks best. You should view sharing knowledge as important as any other process in your organization, including the ones that make money. The trick will be to make sharing knowledge less a formal obligation and more something that people are interested in doing. Most people are glad to share suggestions unless the company has squelched that desire by adding layer after layer of formal processes, many delays, checkpoints, and approvals.

Bottom Line

The more structure an organization has, the less room people have to grow and improve how they contribute. Structure is for safety, convenience, consistency, control, and the like. Cautious companies hire people who meet HR's job descriptions and otherwise fit into the corporate cogs and wheels. This works fine to get the normal work done but not so fine when creativity, innovation, and change are needed.

The bottom line is that organizational structure rarely stimulates change. Engaged people make change happen. Your company cannot build a change structure strictly following anyone's model; your company has to create its own path by learning how to support people who reach outside themselves.

Doesn't it make logical and emotional sense that people drive change, not systems? Get employees engaged; support them and set them free. To the degree your company can do this, your company will get the best from its people.

A Few Undercurrents

CHANGE IS...

Change management is the churning of thoughtful planning and unintended consequences, many of them emotional. We must accept that and be attentive and responsive.

We should stick our feet deeper into the currents of change, into what Herbert Blumer called symbolic interactionism. One of the best at continuous adjustments is Costco, the giant warehouse store. It practically shouts:

> "Come in, come in. We've changed again. You'll find little in its usual place; there is no usual place. We find you so many bargains that we must stick them wherever we can. We scour the world just for you, bargains, quality, quantity, you name it, and we'll find it and sell it to you cheap. Forgive our disarray. This is for you."

Sometimes change represents a relentless search for value. Costco sells us on the ever-changing inventory and the ever-changing arrangement of products. Customers marvel at how well they find so many bargains. They can accept not being able to find something because if often means the item is somewhere else and will be found, it has been replaced by something better and cheaper, or it is such a bargain they are temporarily out of stock. Change is an asset, telling us how diligently they are providing what we want for less.

Some change is so constant that it becomes meaningless to the consumer. "New" and "Improved" on detergent packaging fade into the background. Other changes are an affront to tradition. "New" on a classic soda can is an insult and is rejected.

Changes, major or minor, all have impact. Some can be quickly forgotten and often are as mere inconveniences, or they can fester and bring continued and growing annoyance. A simple change can swell into a symbolic insult. Over the next few pages are brief stories of what swirls under the surface of change and what must be avoided, or at least noticed and mitigated.

The Grinches Who Stole Christmas

Let's say your company put up holiday decorations this year. January second came on a Monday. Facilities went around cleaning up the trees, garlands, snowmen, and whatever else remained from the celebrations. No one had prior notice; two guys just showed up and took away all the materials. Why inform anyone of this simple and necessary housekeeping? This change is like all others: there is more going on than we notice. Employees observing this carnage will say to one another, "This is sad," and be thinking, "I wish they would have left the decorations up for a few more days," or "I would have preferred to take the decorations down myself," and then "Just another example of not being considered about what's going on."

Yes, even this nonevent is a symbolic demonstration of 1) how easily employees can feel slighted and 2) how a simple administrative decision can create the wrong message and 3) how quickly a reasonable action can produce an *us* against *them* mentality.

Unless changes, big and small, make logical and emotional sense you are diluting your organization's ability to foster effective change.

No More Donuts?

I worked for a company that had a monthly managers' meeting. Many of us arrived early to grab a favorite donut and a cup of coffee. Also available were yogurt, apples, bran muffins, tea, and juice. We appreciated this collegial gesture from the company, partly because the meeting was mandatory (useful meetings don't have to be mandatory). One day I arrived to find that the wide range of food and drinks was no longer available, just coffee, tea, and bottled water. There was no advance notice of the change. I was irritated and resentful and I learned others were too. We knew we had to cut costs, but this seemed to be a cheesy way to save a few bucks. Had we known how desperate the need was and what other sacrifices people were making, heck, we may have suggested to cut back on the goodies ourselves, but we weren't included in the discussion.

Did the change make logical sense? Who knows? How much did it make emotional sense? Zero. It cost the organization much more in ill-will from the affected managers than they saved in dollars. Small-minded employees? Maybe. Normal response? Yes.

Hello? Hello? Anyone There?

A few of my favorite print magazines are not keeping up with my deteriorating vision. Actually, the problem is a combination of aging vision and seemingly new and young graphic artists increasing the size of photographs and decreasing the size of text and printing dark text on dark colors and light text on light colors. It looks great. I just can't read it.

I sent comments to four different customer service departments via email, expecting a reply saying they were sorry for my difficulty and maybe offering a suggestion or two. No reply. I imagine that either the recipient in customer service felt it was an editorial problem and forwarded it or that it was a dumb problem and ignored my email. Since I am no longer a favored demographic, I suppose my distress was of little concern to them. I gave them feedback but received none in return. But that is not my point although I do think feedback is vastly underdone.

I wonder about the job satisfaction and sense of purpose of the person who first received my email. He or she evidently was primed not to care about this one individual complaining about the size of print in their magazine. How pervasive is that attitude? Any business, any good business anyway, views complaints as a free, spot-on organizational development department manned by a most treasured resource. A customer complaint is an opportunity to improve in a way that is important to the people who pay the bills. Receiving feedback from customers is a gift, one that should be cherished by the organization. If an organization doesn't care about customer comments, how much can they care about the thoughts and feelings of their workers?

This lack of interest in replying reminds me of the attitude of some busy people who resent receiving an email just saying "thanks." Their stance is they helped someone no big deal, and the email of appreciation only adds clutter to their mailbox. The two seconds to open a thank-you email should be worthwhile. I wonder about people and organizations that want to save time by neglecting human connections. Such sterility may be okay in otherwise fast-moving, exuberant start-ups, but I can't believe minimizing people connections is useful elsewhere, especially in an organization that wants to improve.

A New Boss with Great Ideas

The room was anxiously, mostly positively, awaiting the new boss. He had over twenty years of experience and was highly regarded in the industry. They needed his help after struggling the past four years with high turnover, product delays, and diminishing sales. He would turn things around.

He strode through the doorway on time. Looking sharp in a dark gray suit, he said, "Good morning," as he continued to the front of the room. After a few pleasantries, he got down to his action plan. We would change all areas, he said. It was obvious he knew our problems and obvious he had clear ideas of how to solve them. He went into detail for each of his ideas. The group began to fidget. His machine-gun approach seemed like a power trip, almost taking the stance it was his way or the highway. Some of the audience was thinking he had success where he came from, but at what cost?

Instead of promoting changes, what if he had focused on engagement? He could have told a story about his prior job, made a statement about a problem, and how they worked together to overcome obstacles. After the story, he could have said with his own emotional engagement, "Let's do even better here," and won everybody over. But he didn't. Instead, he went from problem to solution without including us.

A Confession at PCM

Improving reception at Pacific Coast Medical also uncovered one of the frequent unintended consequences of change. After a team meeting, Karen, a receptionist, asked Dr. Hull if she could talk with him. As soon as they sat, Karen began to cry. "It's hard for me to say this but making us into a better team made me want to tell you. I'm afraid one of the receptionists may cause a problem with patient care."

Dr. Hull said, "Tell me more."

"If someone comes in complaining of chest pains, we're supposed to get a nurse immediately. When a patient says that to Abby, she asks them more questions, like any nausea or other symptoms. She's been told how to do it right but hasn't changed. I hate to say it, Abby is a problem, but Sue has known about Abby's behavior for a long time and isn't doing anything about it. No one seems to care if we're doing a good job or not. Making check-in easier is nice, but the lack of real leadership is putting lives at risk."

And so it goes. Once you start effective change, you may be buried in a landslide of opportunities. Fail to respond to them at your peril.

The Un-Change Change

Everyone was looking forward to the new VP. She had been touted as a fortunate catch, having worked for the competition and who now wanted to work for us. Her first day of work was in two weeks. Our old VP had left six months earlier, and I thought we'd never find someone. His temporary replacement, one of our most experienced directors, didn't feel right about taking the job and was clear he didn't want it but did the job well enough that we had the luxury of looking for the best.

We underlings did the prep work, making sure her office was fit for her to hit the ground running, that her calendar was up to date, and her new business cards were ready and waiting. They would have to wait. A week before her arrival, we were told she wouldn't be coming. That was it: "She wouldn't be coming." No reason was given. We all understood that HR or whoever can't go blabbing the details of someone's career, but we got nothing. "She decided not to come," would have been enough, barely, but enough. We were disappointed, sure, but more than that. No one upstairs seemed to care about us. We had hopes. We felt connected. We had conversations. We had expectations. We got nothing. "Ah well, out of the loop again. I guess some things never change."

Nothing Never Happens

These vignettes portray the undercurrents that swirl every day and every night at the workplace and at the dinner table, in every organization, in every group, and in every family. No leader or manager can anticipate the frequency and range of reactions to change but be aware they are happening, everywhere, all the time.

Just as we know people do not, *not* like change, we also know that people do not, *not* react. Nothing never happens. You want your colleagues to react, you want them to care. Just make sure you don't do nothing about it when they do care and they do react.

How Will We Know?

Businesspeople know the importance of measurement. How can you know how something is working unless you measure it? Business experts call it metrics. Some organizations, especially ones using Lean Thinking or Six Sigma, have war rooms with every wall covered with diagrams, graphs, lists, and hundreds if not thousands of numbers detailing what is happening throughout the business. They forget or don't know, that true knowledge comes from "seeing with your own eyes," and not relying on abstract and perhaps outdated numbers. The same truth about metrics applies to people.

As you think about developing change metrics, consider the relative importance of the metrics of:

- Working to improve a process
- Promoting the logical and emotional sense of change
- Supporting and developing the people who make the change a reality

What is the best balance of these three metrics? Of these metrics and all others? How do you know?

Change is complex, people reactions lead to people interactions, uncertainty, apprehension, misperception, and misunderstanding. As we cut through this tangle, how will we know we are doing it right on the people side? All we need to do is ask in one form or another, "How is it going?" to find out.

The one thing OD people who advocate personality profiling got right is the importance of emotional reactions. Our position has been to avoid setting up situations that promote negative reactions and when they occur anyway, legitimize them, explore them, get to the root causes, and, together with those affected, get rid of them. You need to talk, and you need to listen.

For any change, assume people are experiencing feelings, good, bad, and indifferent. Ask them, "How is this change affecting you?" Don't defend, don't explain, and don't solve anything. Listen. The likely causes of distress are misunderstanding the change, not agreeing with the change, or being personally and negatively affected by the change. These are normal and legitimate responses. The undercurrents of change mandate a competent response from leaders.

These are some first change management questions to explore:

- How do you see the issues?
- What outcomes are you seeking?
- Were team goals set and agreed to by all?
- Did all team members have a say in team functioning?
- Did team members receive the identified personal rewards?
- Did managers include all employees in the HST process?
- Were the issue and goal mutually defined?
- How was the solution identified? Agreed to by all?
- Was communication sufficient? How do you know?
- How much feedback was there for each HST step?

And these for improved sustainability:

- How is the organization improved with this change?
- Any negative outcomes?
- Was there universal engagement for the change? If not, why not?
- Were there obvious benefits for each employee?
- How did this change develop employees?
- Did the change identify other important issues?

Every step of the HST model has a built-in "revise as needed." No change will be perfect. If participants know that their voices will be heard at the beginning, middle, and end of the change, all will be as good as it can be. If the cultural attitude is "Let's do our best to make this happen and fix anything we need to along the way," people will soon develop the attitude that the critical change emotions of *inclusion*, *comfort*, and *excitement* are a reality and undercurrents will be brought to the surface and addressed. You can't do better than that.

FINAL THOUGHTS

A Few Ideas to Consider

There are four phases of organizational development. They are:

1. Discovering the need to make a change
2. Deciding on the change
3. Implementing the change
4. Sustaining the change or doing something else

Discover the need to make a change by identifying the gap between what is now and what should be. Decide what, if any, change to make using HST, which also helps make logical and emotional sense of the change. Implementing and sustaining change is done through teams and supportive leadership. This is what must happen for effective organizational change. The details of how you do this are up to you and others in your organization.

The Basic Idea

The Japanese saying "None of us is as smart as all of us" sounds good, but in most places isn't true. More likely it's "too many cooks spoil the broth."

I wrote articles for one company, who edited them by committee. My most clear, concise, and impactful words were bowdlerized into the ordinary, rendering them no more tasty than soggy cereal. People working together are often inefficient and ineffective. On a well-functioning team, however, everyone takes part and contributes. That's the basic idea. All of us are smarter only if we can work well together. Usually, that isn't the case. Transparent tools and models change that.

HURDLES AND CONCERNS

If our ability to manage change is as inefficient as most think, we must avoid making mistakes and erroneous assumptions. We must be as efficient and effective as possible. Our focus has been on building trust, assuming that trust, once built and maintained, can smooth rough spots and build bridges over errors and omissions. Transparency helps us do that. We also respect people's need for logical and emotional sense in what they do and are asked to do and asked to trust.

At the same time, however, change isn't easy and is ripe for well-meaning mistakes, misleading ideas, and outright dumb ideas. There have been countless efforts to understand the people side of implementing change. They can become hurdles and concerns, not assets. Some have championed the concept that change is so odious that only by applying psychiatric type treatment for grief reactions can we overcome the trauma. Others promote applying the power of psychological tests to understand the complexities of people. Many focus on the rigidities of company culture while perhaps an equal number are split on declaring the effect of leaders as the major force to be blamed or to be hailed as the secret to success.

Fans of the complexity of change tout Everett Rogers' adoption process of knowledge, persuasion, decision, implementation, and confirmation. The adoption of this process is often depicted in the labels attached to standard deviations on a bell curve: Innovators, Early Adopters, Early Majority, Late Majority, and Laggards. These labels become dysfunctional if leaders believe that for every hundred people in an organization, thirty-four will comprise the late majority and should be helped in various ways. Categorizing people and then creating helpful interventions for these categories is an unnecessary and counterproductive complication to change efforts.

Another concern is using models with little or no actual relevance. I cringe when I see the so-called change curve based on Kübler-Ross's grief reaction, the presenter blithely explaining how the pit of despair awaits the unwary as if it were true. This person is creating a new problem, one that need not exist except for a penchant for applying pseudoscience. If we want to simplify the complexities of people, we must be darn sure to do it right and not lose the essence we are trying to capture. To simplify means to be clearer, not to disguise what is true under a blanket of erroneous thinking.

Elisabeth Kübler-Ross and her portrayal of someone facing a terminal illness does not belong in the work setting and is not the classic response employees experience when facing change yet is promoted anyway. If you like this approach, including the change curve with the "pit of despair" at the bottom (which makes a dramatic PowerPoint slide), read Kübler-Ross's writings on her system, and you will know better. She said her model is not all-inclusive, that the order can change and, she emphasized, grief is an individualized experience. How such a wobbly platform could become an accepted way of understanding organizational change is beyond me.

Psychometrics also seems to be an organizational change magnet. The Myers-Briggs Type Indicator and similar vehicles for stuffing people into boxes are semi-science (and another potential embarrassment for change leaders) and at worst is a biased and prejudicial stereotyping of unique human beings. I am concerned about using a method based on debunked psychoanalytic thinking or unsubstantiated theories. Using such tools is not how to make sense of change for the people involved. If you're doing that, please stop. Before you're tempted to use psychosocial instruments, check out validity and reliability studies by neutral parties.

I searched for independent validation of the MBTI, for example, and couldn't find any. But I uncovered other OD practitioners who wondered about validity and reliability and who also couldn't find such data. I fear users of most change psychometrics receive just enough training to be confident and not enough to be competent. Additionally, I've taken the MBTI three times, resulting in three different scores, which gave me pause: isn't personality supposed to be stable? Even if the MBTI proves to be a reliable and valid measure, what good is it to put people into categories? And in only one spectrum, as if this approach somehow has precedence over all others.

Here are a few opinions on the MBTI matter:

From Adam Grant: "… we all need to recognize that four letters don't do justice to anyone's identity. So leaders, consultants, counselors, coaches, and teachers, join me in delivering this message: MBTI, I'm breaking up with you. It's not me. It's you."

https://www.psychologytoday.com/blog/give-and-take/201309/goodbye-mbti-the-fad-won-t-die

David J. Pittenger: "I believe that MBTI attempts to force the complexities of human personality into an artificial and limiting classification scheme. The focus on the "typing" of people reduces the attention paid to the unique qualities and potential of each individual."

http://www.indiana.edu/~jobtalk/Articles/develop/mbti.pdf

And the ever-popular Wikipedia: "Most of the research supporting the MBTI's validity has been produced by the Centre for Applications of Psychological Type, an organization run by the Myers-Briggs Foundation, and published in the Centre's own journal, the *Journal of Psychological Type*, raising questions of independence, bias, and conflict of interest. Independent sources have called the test 'bullshit', "little more than a Chinese fortune cookie, 'pretty much meaningless' and 'the fad that won't die'".

Though the MBTI resembles some psychological theories, it is generally classified as pseudoscience, especially as pertains to its supposed predictive abilities.

https://en.wikipedia.org/wiki/My-ers%E2%80%93Briggs_Type_Indicator

I believe you will appreciate the folly of categorizing people. It is true such inventories make humans more understandable and available to targeted interventions, but so does stereotyping by race, religion, and gender. Measures such as DISC and Personal Styles that identify simple behavioral tendencies can be useful if they celebrate and support differences and don't assume to plumb the intricacies of personality.

I have used Harnessing the Speed of Thought for over forty years because it worked. I continually looked toward research for scientific support of what I was observing. It has scientific support, including recent findings that the brain tends to mis-trust novel experiences, assuming that they could be dangerous. All the more reason to slow the thought process and make it transparent.

Teams

I'm a Patrick Lencioni fan. Although the Four-Part Teaming Model was developed independently of his material, it is interesting how well the model addresses his five dysfunctions:

Lencioni model worries about…	Williams model addresses through…
Absence of trust	Membership, influence on the team
Fear of conflict	Influence on the team
Lack of commitment	Compelling task, membership
Avoidance of accountability	Membership, influence on the team
Inattention to results	Compelling task, membership, personal reward

The only place I know where Rudy wrote about his model is in *Mistake-Proofing Leadership* which we wrote together.

Lean Thinking and the Seven People Assets

Lean Thinking, developed from the Toyota Production System, is the attempt to reduce waste in production processes, specifically these seven wastes: transportation, inventory, movement, waiting, over-processing, overproduction, and defects. There were a few forward thinkers who wanted to add people issues to Lean Thinking, including Bob Emiliani of Central Connecticut State University and Norman Bodek of PCS Press. Initially, the tactic was to add a people waste to the classic seven production wastes. This eighth waste was variations of underutilizing human potential, such as not speaking up at meetings and ignoring creative ideas. There was also interest in Toyota's "Respect for People" initiative. I investigated these ideas and the thoughts of many others studying the people side of Lean. My quest was to determine if Lean Thinking ideas could improve people interactions. Toyota's respect for people turned out to be a focus on people only to improve production processes and not to improve people interactions. And adding only one people waste to encompass the whole of human experience at work seemed unduly limiting.

In *Lean Thinking 4.0,* I proposed Seven People Assets that should be enhanced to harmonize with the seven production wastes. This one-two punch would significantly improve continuous improvement efforts. I believe the same is necessary for any organizational development; process improvement must be combined with people inclusion and enhancement.

If you want to create an organization that is efficient and can make change easier and more successful, you can enhance what you already have in place. Specifically, in these areas:

1. Teamwork
2. Leadership
3. Communication
4. Problem-solving
5. Engagement
6. Rewards
7. Knowledge

These were the seven people areas I found that best complemented the classic seven wastes of Lean Thinking for process improvement and the equally important people factors of change. Most Lean organizations make the same mistake in promoting change that other organizations do, they focus on improving processes and disregard or minimize the importance of improving people interactions. The value of the Seven People Assets is to support and develop people at the same time process waste is being reduced.

If your organization is pursuing Lean Thinking or perhaps Six Sigma, you may benefit from a more structured way of supporting the people side of change. The Seven People Assets comprise the most important areas to enhance how people work with one another so that Lean process changes can be sustained. It seems a small step to apply the value of the Seven People Assets to all organizational development. These assets already exist in every organization and prove useful in ensuring change makes logical and emotional sense.

Problem Solving

Care must be taken when using the core HST problem-solving model. Say, for example, your company creates ten widgets a day. Marketing finds that demand is twenty widgets a day. The issue you define, the gap, is "We produce ten widgets a day, demand is twenty." What should your goal be? If you thought, "meet demand by producing twenty widgets a day," you did not harness your speed of thought. You proffered a solution.

A goal might be to "determine the optimal output and achieve that number." Assessing competition, expansion costs, etc., might support something other than completely meeting demand. The wrong goal limits opportunities. Making twelve widgets of better quality and charging more might be the way to go.

Take all the time needed to completely analyze and understand the issue and goal. It isn't as easy and as quick as your brain would like.

People in Organizations

The only reason businesses exist is to meet human needs and desires, from new cars to an elegant dinner to saving the rain forests. I believe there is no reason to ignore the needs and desires of the people working for the business just for the sake of business. Healthy organizational change comes down to individuals distinguishing between "do I have to?" and "do I want to?" Persuasion, which seems to be the popular tactic, eventually weakens and fails. When individuals decide "I want to," then wonderful things can happen.

So many companies tout their people as vital to their success in providing their customers with the best products and services. And so many tout their "teams" as the reason for success. Unless employees really are on teams, this touting is empty for customers, for employees and for the organization. High-performing teams and the effective leaders who support them make the difference.

The HST model for change should not fade into just another flavor of the month. It is not a template, not an add-on, but a direct reflection of how the brain functions and how people can effectively work together. The HST model for change enhances how people can understand and assimilate each other's ideas and points of view. Put people first, change second and everybody wins.

Resources

For more complete information on Harnessing the Speed of Thought and Teamwork:

Transparent Management, Robert Brown (2008, 2011)

To learn more about how the mind works:

What Is Thought, Eric B. Baum (2004)

Thinking Fast and Slow, Daniel Kahneman (2011)

Blink, Malcolm Gladwell (2007)

If you want to know more about my approach to organizational change:

The People Side of Lean Thinking, Robert Brown (2012)

Lean Thinking 4.0, Robert Brown (2018)

My favorite John Kotter book (which presents his now-famous eight steps, his emphasis on story and "see-feel-change"):

The Heart of Change, John Kotter (2001; there is a newer edition)

For the book that started everything for me (although focused on education, his analytic approach can be useful everywhere):

Educational System Planning, Roger A. Kaufman (1972)

For my take on customer service and employee engagement (a story about a burned-out executive finding inspiration in a computer-crammed house in Scotland):

Earn Their Loyalty, Robert Brown (2011)

Another book you may find useful (a fictional account of leaders attending what I consider the best leadership training on earth):

Mistake-Proofing Leadership, Rudy Williams and Robert Brown (2008, 2010, 2019)

Another resource you may find interesting is an off-the-wall exploration of how companies are organized and how they should change if they wish to survive and thrive as long as possible):

New Darwinian Laws Every Business Should Know, Patrick Edmonds and Robert Brown (2016)

A few more of my favorites:

The Five Dysfunctions of a Team, Patrick Lencioni (2002)

How to Win Friends and Influence People, Dale Carnegie (new edition, 2010)

The Essential Drucker: The Best of Sixty Years of Peter Drucker's Essential Writings on Management, Peter Drucker (2008)

Crucial Conversations: Tools for Talking When Stakes Are High, Second Edition, Kerry Patterson and Joseph Grenny (2011)

Influencer: The New Science of Leading Change, Kerry Patterson (2013, 2nd edition)

The SPEED of TRUST: The One Thing That Changes Everything, Stephen M .R. Covey and Stephen R. Covey (2008)

The Baptist Health Care Journey to Excellence: Creating a Culture that WOWs!, Al Stubblefield (2004)

Up the Organization: How to Stop the Corporation from Stifling People and Strangling Profits, Robert C. Townsend and Warren Bennis (2007, new edition)

Communicating Change, TJ and Sandar Larkin (1994)

The Mind Club, Daniel M. Wegner and Kurt Gray (2016)

The Tides of Mind, David Gelernter (2016)

Being Wrong, Kathryn Schulz (2010)

Sapiens, Yuval Noah Harari (2015)

ACKNOWLEDGMENTS

I have made it a practice to send Brian Weisel of the Salina Regional Medical Center the initial draft of my management books for his thoughts. He unfailingly provides the right blend of overview and detailed notes that point me in the right direction. My second alpha reader for this project was Carlos Venegas of OfficeRocket.com. His wise words of keeping it simple made for a lot more work and a much better presentation of ideas. (He also loaned me his broken flashlight image.)

I met George Mante at a conference, since then he has been a significant support as a beta reader with solid and perceptive ideas. His friend Phil Jones went the extra mile and provided me with a detailed analysis of the points I wanted to make and led me in a better direction.

Joe Mitchell read one of my other books and was kind enough to email me his thoughts. He was also kind enough to become a beta reader for this book. He added his considerable leadership experience to evaluate the text and made a substantial contribution to its value.

Former coworkers Rudy Williams, Marlenna Peppler, Steve Stahl, and Thomas Nielsen were a formidable team directing my growth in OD. I cannot thank them enough for my joy of working with them. Rudy, of course, is the author of the Four-Part Teaming Model and has been a kind and supportive mentor for more than a decade.

David Antrobus has been the editor for my last few books and continues to find enough to improve in my writing to remind me of how much more there is to learn.

Shirley Miles-Wantanabe has read many of my books, is a friend, and was a coworker. Her enthusiasm for my work has been a force in my efforts to search for the correct words and the best sentences to effectively convey a good idea. I work hard not to let her down.

My brother-in-law Danny Williams has become the final arbiter of whether a manuscript to ready to become a book.

And my wife Deena; I cannot imagine life without her support.

About the Author

Bob Brown, president of Collective Wisdom, Inc., has been a performance enhancement consultant for over forty years. If you are applying the ideas in this book, Bob is available for 2-3-day consults where he talks with people, creates impromptu workshops and seminars, coaches, and otherwise enables you to improve your organization. He also is a popular keynote speaker.

He has a doctorate in psychology and is a certified Lean Leader.

Bob lives with his wife and various animals, wild and domestic, north of Seattle.

You can reach him at collectivewisdom2020@gmail.com

Also available:

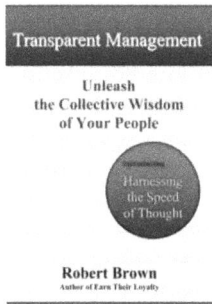

Transparent Management

Unleash
the Collective Wisdom
of Your People

Harnessing
the Speed
of Thought

Robert Brown
Author of Earn Their Loyalty

The introduction to Harnessing the Speed of Thought and the Four-Part Teaming Model plus other tools for good management and organizational development.

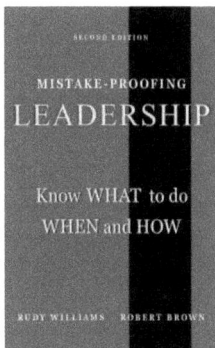

SECOND EDITION

MISTAKE-PROOFING

LEADERSHIP

Know WHAT to do
WHEN and HOW

RUDY WILLIAMS   ROBERT BROWN

The story of a group of leaders meeting weekly to improve their leadership skills. Join them to experience months long training in just a few hours. Tools are presented and fully explained so you can begin using them immediately.

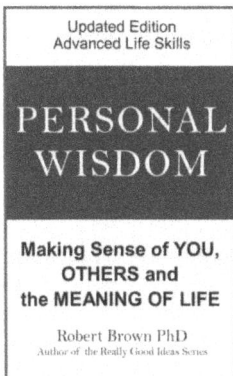

Updated Edition
Advanced Life Skills

PERSONAL
WISDOM

Making Sense of YOU,
OTHERS and
the MEANING OF LIFE

Robert Brown PhD
Author of the Really Good Ideas Series

A comprehensive look at the value of a single life, yours. No one, not God or anyone, wants you to simply rehash what has gone on before. Your existence is unique, and your life should be the same.

People interacting with one another is the backbone of business and is the logical next target for the power of Lean Thinking. Using Lean tools in areas where they have not been used before and using human interaction tools that are not Lean tools, in Lean ways.

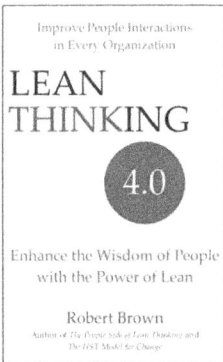

Lean Thinking can improve production processes. Brown presents Lean tools and concepts that can improve the processes of people interactions. Meetings will improve. Leadership will be more effective. Teams will run like clockwork.

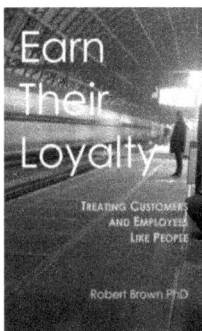

Allowing employees to handle customers any way they please is letting a loose cannon determine the fate of the business. As inconvenient as it may seem, customers and employees are still people, and should be treated like people.

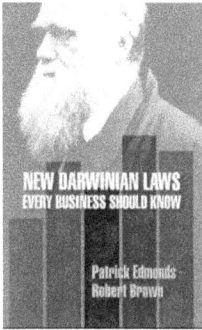

NEW DARWINIAN LAWS
EVERY BUSINESS SHOULD KNOW

Patrick Edmonds
Robert Brown

No company can live forever, but success comes to those that can best adapt: Not the biggest, not the strongest, not the fastest, not the smartest and certainly not the oldest. New Darwinian Laws explores what makes a business able to adapt better than its competitors.